Please Don't Shoot the Messenger!

HOW TO TALK
TO DEMANDING BOSSES,
CLUELESS COLLEAGUES,
TOUGH CUSTOMERS,
AND DIFFICULT CLIENTS
WITHOUT LOSING YOUR COOL
(OR YOUR JOB!)

Dr. Gary S. Goodman

CB
CONTEMPORARY BOOKS

Library of Congress Cataloging-in-Publication Data

Goodman, Dr. Gary S.
    Please don't shoot the messenger! : how to talk to demanding bosses, clueless
colleagues, tough customers, and difficult clients without losing your cool (or
your job!) / Dr. Gary S. Goodman.
        p.   cm.
    Includes index.
    ISBN 0-8092-2520-4
    1. Negotiation in business.   I. Title.
HD58.6.G663   2000
658.4'052—dc21   99-38814
                                                                              CIP

Cover design by Monica Baziuk
Interior design by Rattray Design

Published by Contemporary Books
A division of NTC/Contemporary Publishing Group, Inc.
4255 West Touhy Avenue, Lincolnwood (Chicago), Illinois 60712-1975 U.S.A.
Printed in the United States of America
International Standard Book Number: 0-8092-2520-4
00 01 02 03 04 05 MV 15 14 13 12 11 10 9 8 7 6 5 4 3 2 1

This book is dedicated to my wife, best friend, and
colleague, Dr. Deanne Honeyman Goodman, and
to our wonderful daughter,
Amanda Leigh Goodman.

Contents

Acknowledgments

I WOULD LIKE to thank my editor, Danielle Egan-Miller, and my project editor, Heidi Bresnahan, of NTC/Contemporary Books for believing in this book and for bringing it to you, the reader.

I would also like to thank my consulting clients and all of the librarians and booksellers for putting this book into your hands.

1

Mastering the Psychology of Conflict Prevention and Conflict Management

Do you feel you take home too many unresolved, work-related stresses and resentments?

When dealing with aggressive people, do you find you give in too often and give away too much?

Do you ever automatically snap back when people snap at you?

Do you need better control over your anger when you're in difficult situations?

I

Would you like to smile more, frown less, and be able to shrug off what you can't change about other people?

When you're in conflict situations, do you ever feel short of breath?

After a nasty encounter, do you evaluate yourself too harshly?

Are defensive people especially hard to deal with?

Are you ever reluctant to act assertively when dealing with difficult people?

Would you like to feel more positive and upbeat, come what may?

IF YOU FOUND yourself answering yes to any of these questions, this chapter is for you.

In this chapter you'll learn about: our four predictable and often problematic responses to conflicts; how to manage your inner conflicts; the ABCs of reprogramming your emotional reactions; how to use laughter; how to breathe like a yogi; the value of walking, hitting, and kicking away your blues; how to avoid self-downing; how to take the long view of events; how to keep business matters from becoming too personal; how to recognize and reduce defensiveness in ourselves and others; how "justice" happens; how to pack profits into the next deal; how to flash assertiveness; how to act like water; how to take a vacation from job stresses; how L-E-A-R-N-I-N-G is the best revenge; and how to stay positive, come what may.

*   *   *   *   *   *   *

A group of old high school buddies were gathered around a candlelit dinner at a trendy New York restaurant. Alan, who had always been considered a nice, but ineffectual guy, lamented over being a perennial screwup. "Bad things are always happening to me," he whined.

Just as his pals were nodding in agreement and consoling him, they smelled something funny. A waitress gently tapped Alan on the shoulder and whispered, "Pardon me, but I think your hair is on fire." Apparently, Alan had leaned back on his chair while emoting, and a candle singed his dangling locks.

Having thought quickly, the waitress was wise for not screaming "Fire!" in a crowded restaurant. She broke the bad news with as much composure as anyone could hope for and thus prevented a chaotic stampede for the exits.

The business world is filled with challenging circumstances where we have to break bad news or express uncomfortable information to people who don't want to hear it. Generally, we would prefer not to do it, because it's painful and most of us dislike conflict. We're also concerned that if we break bad news to someone, that person might be tempted to seek retribution by "killing the messenger."

How This Book Will Help

This book will help you overcome your reluctance to speak up and assert your rightful agenda. You'll learn the mechanics of crafting powerful, clear, and professional messages that get your point across with as little nasty fallout as possible.

Equally important, you'll learn how to equip yourself with the best attitudes for handling workplace stress and tensions that arise from conflict. This first chapter will point out what you need to tell yourself before you can feel comfortable telling other people what they need to know. It will show you how to remain calm and tranquil, as well as help you master the psychology of conflict prevention and management.

How People Normally Approach Conflict Management

Have you ever had an impassioned argument with a customer, a coworker, or your boss, and muttered to yourself: "We would have a wonderful relationship if it weren't for you!"? Possibly, you've told yourself: "If they would only be different, if they would only change, be nicer, see things my way, and just give me what I want, everything could be so perfect!"

You are completely normal to think these thoughts. Most of us think them most of the time. In fact, when we're in conflict situations, we invest tons of energy defending our decisions and our viewpoints.

As our disagreements fester, our egos seek to produce results that portray our positions in the most favorable light. We can become more interested in *winning* than in doing the most productive thing. So what started out as a minor skirmish can quickly escalate into a major war.

Isn't There a Better Way?

You might have wondered, aren't there better ways to prevent and manage our business conflicts? Can't we develop a certain amount of practical eloquence in order to reduce tensions and get back on track?

Happily, there are many things we can do. I'm going to share some helpful and productive ways of understanding the psychology of conflict. I'll give you a conceptual understanding of what happens when we're in states of conflict, both internally when we're stressed out, and externally when we don't seem to get along with other people. Then I'll conclude this chapter by providing you with practical tips for making your disagreements and misunderstandings less bruising and distracting.

Conflict Is Normal Despite What Many People Believe

In some families nobody ever openly fights with anybody else. They might even abide by a rule such as, "There is to be no yelling in this household!" People who make these decrees believe they can preempt major disagreements simply by legislating them away.

Trying to live up to a norm of constant tranquillity is very uncomfortable—for a simple reason. It's impossible to achieve, because on this earthly plane conflict is a normal occurrence. What is abnormal is the idea that conflict is abnormal.

Therapists will tell you that healthy families air their disagreements—at least occasionally. They let off steam and encourage members to have occasional purges of pent-up dissatisfactions. Doing this prevents the harboring of submerged hostilities that can erupt and may become permanently damaging.

The same principle applies to companies and their employees. They need to get whatever is bothering them out into the open, at least occasionally. And they need to do so without hating themselves or feeling that they're mad or bad for doing so.

Our Four Predictable Responses to Conflict

You've heard that we can be our own worst enemies. This is absolutely true when it comes to handling friction with other people. When we're about to respond to someone who is obviously angry, we are altogether too quick to do one of four things:

1. We may avoid the person, hoping that he or she will just go away and conveniently take the disagreement with him or her. This is wishful thinking. Unattended hostilities can slowly simmer and build up destructive potential until they erupt like Mount St. Helens.

2. We might rush to offer a compromise, but this, too, can backfire. Bill was asked by his company to investigate the theft of products from the warehouse. After a lot of spade work, he discovered that one of the boss's relatives was responsible. He wrote a report identifying the perpetrator and submitted it to his superior, who was incensed. "We can't accuse the boss's nephew of being a thief! Find another explanation, or simply report that you couldn't turn up anything," Bill's supervisor counseled.

Bill had to decide whether to tell the truth and possibly be fired for doing so, or to compromise the truth and his principles, and thereby try to maintain his connection with the firm. After studying the situation, Bill saw that compromising wasn't always the best policy. He chose to disclose the facts.

3. We might simply fight back when we feel we've been provoked. You'll meet many people in business who have hair-trigger tempers when dealing with others. The second they feel they have been crossed, they lash out, as if to say, "Don't tread on me!" Occasionally this works,

and by showing some anger they can preclude further encroachments. It's akin to a dog issuing a warning bark before it bites. The bark, while appearing to be a hostile act, can actually prevent even greater harm from befalling potential combatants.

However, if such people always lash out or counter anger with anger, they are undoubtedly going to escalate hostilities with a number of adversaries. And, as in warfare, once escalation has occurred, it can be extremely difficult to de-escalate.

4. Some purported peacemakers try to coddle angry people. "Now, now," they might whisper, "this is nothing to get upset over." Of course, their goals may be noble, but if they try to tell some angry folks there's no reason to be miffed, the hotheads will argue about that as well! So such coddling can end up adding fuel to the fire, which splits into two blazes: the original dispute and a debate about the appropriateness of the dispute.

The Greatest Conflicts You'll Manage Will Be Inside of You

You may not be able to control what people say to you, but to a large extent you *can* control how *you* react to what they say. We have an important duty to do as little harm to ourselves as possible, both professionally and psychologically, as we deal with interpersonal difficulties.

I'm going to explain the psychology of remaining sane, and even calm, as you approach challenging disagreements. The methodology I'll present to you has its origins in ancient Greece, so it represents good, old-fashioned wisdom. It has also been updated by psychologist Albert Ellis in recent years, and he named it rational-emotive psychology. (I studied with Ellis at the University of California, Riverside, and I've read a number of his books.) In essence, he says the following sequence of thoughts occurs to most of us as we grow angry:

There is an activating event. Let's say you're at work, and an associate looks at your desk and snickers, "A messy desk is the mark of genius, huh?" Obviously, the person is joking with you, but there might also be criticism in the message, right?

The next thing that happens is you interpret the activating event by filtering it through your belief system. If you have thin skin when it comes to being criticized, you might think: "Who is *he* to bug me about my desk? He's not so organized. In fact, he's a pig. Just look at how he dresses!" In other words, you may foster the belief that you shouldn't be criticized and when you are, you should criticize right back. Or you might entertain the belief that it's awful and it hurts you whenever people criticize you or make jokes at your expense.

The final event that occurs in this reaction sequence is an emotional consequence. You choose to feel a certain way, based upon the perception and evaluation of the activating event. "I feel awful," you might say, or you could tell yourself, "He hurt me with that nasty remark."

The key to this process is that it works like ABC, according to Ellis. The activating event triggers our belief system, which in turn triggers an emotion in us. So if we want to control our emotional outcomes, we can choose to modify our beliefs that are getting in our way.

For example, I'm in customer service for a mutual fund company. The stock market starts swooning, sending my company's shares into the toilet. Scared and angry customers call up and demand to know why their assets are plummeting in value. In fact, they are so peeved, they use profanity with me, which I find awful. Every day I leave work with a headache and feeling totally stressed out. What can I do? After all, it is the customers who are swearing at me. If they use language to victimize me, shouldn't I react as a victim would?

Absolutely not. Using the rational-emotive model, we might see that we can't prevent four-letter words from escaping customers' lips. Even if we proclaimed, "You can't swear at me!" some bozos would still do it, if only out of spite.

How to Reprogram Your Emotional Reactions

What we *can* control is our belief systems and, therefore, our feelings about the swearing. If I become outraged and nearly apoplectic because someone is cussing at me, it isn't because this language is so inherently awful. It's only words, right? (Remember we learned in childhood, "Sticks and stones may break my bones but names will never hurt me"?)

The problem lies in what I tell myself about the goodness or badness of certain words. If I walk around with the belief "It's awful whenever any customer swears at me," guess how I will feel the next time it happens? Wonderful? No way! I'm simply setting myself up to feel awful. By choosing to foster this extremely negative belief about profanity, I'm ensuring that I'll get really mad whenever I'm exposed to it.

By the same token, I can change my emotional reaction to a stimulus by changing my beliefs. First I have to ask myself, "What am I telling myself about this activating event?" The answer will be I'm telling myself that it's awful whenever anybody swears at me.

Why is it awful, instead of simply being uncomfortable? Who says being cussed at has to feel awful? Well, in truth, many folks have been brought up to believe that swearing at another person is the verbal equivalent of using physical violence. Swearing violates one of the norms of polite society.

Also, we can have negative reactions because being sworn at can make us feel threatened—as if physical harm might befall us next. This may be a fundamental, animalistic, self-protective response. The fear may release adrenaline, which could enable us to fight or flee, depending upon what we think is appropriate.

But in the ordinary compass of business events, we're not going to physically be at risk. So we can safely adopt a less extreme reaction to profanity. By implanting into our belief system the idea that profanity is mildly uncomfortable, we'll quickly get over profanity when we hear it.

Thus we can reprogram our reactions—our emotional consequences. Let me offer another example of how this can work in everyday life. When I started doing seminars through universities across the country, participants would approach me during breaks and ask, "How much would it cost to bring you in to speak at my company?" Frankly, I wasn't prepared for such questions, so I didn't know how to respond. I probably mumbled something like, "Well, that would depend upon what you want me to do, and how long it will take."

I also felt uncomfortable, for some reason. After doing a little bit of analysis, I determined that I felt peculiar because I saw myself more as a university professor than as a speaker for hire. I quickly changed that limiting belief, and I resolved to perceive myself effectively performing both roles.

From then on, whenever people asked me to speak, I had a clear and positive answer for them, and as a result my consulting practice boomed. Until I addressed my peculiar belief about speaking inquiries, I was stuck in a pattern of producing suboptimal consequences for myself and my potential clients.

We need to appreciate that we're not hardwired to have specific emotional responses to most interpersonal situations. We can choose our reactions. I chose to enjoy the inquiries I received and to treat them as the compliments that they were.

You can choose to remain calm and tranquil in the face of highly emotional provocations. Much of the remaining portion of this chapter will provide you with some excellent responses to ensure that you'll keep your head, even while others are losing theirs.

Learn to Enjoy Everything. Life doesn't come with an operating manual. Surely, parents try to educate their children to cope and to enjoy themselves while being productive members of society. But really, we're on our own when it comes to deriving pleasure or pain from our experiences.

We should try to be grateful for the way things happen. This is a way of saying that we should accept the bad in the same spirit as we accept the good.

Even if we seem to be deluged with responsibilities, deadlines, and pressing personalities, we can find ways to derive value and satisfaction from our situations. Even if we merely appreciate that "I've never had it this tough before!" we enhance our potential for being thoroughly alive.

Make Yourself Laugh. Do you know where the best comedians come from? Poor and dysfunctional backgrounds. It's true. They learn to turn the surrounding apparent waste into treasure. Rodney Dangerfield is an example. Hailing from very modest beginnings, he recalled in a routine he did on the "Tonight Show":

"In my house, we were so poor that we couldn't afford to put cheese into our mousetraps. So we used pictures of cheese. You know what we caught? Pictures of mice!"

You can do the same thing. Whenever your feelings of stress ratchet upward, become aware of it. Then try to see the humor in your circumstances. Believe me, there is something funny about nearly everything. When you can make yourself smile, you'll puncture the negative aura that seems to lurk all around you.

Make Somebody Else Laugh. I've found that if I can make somebody else smile, I'll relax immediately thereafter. I suspect that this works because laughter really is a tonic, even if the laughter we evoke isn't our own.

Also, when we inspire laughter, we can feel good about the fact that we've lightened someone else's day. Making a person's day is like doing that person a favor. And it doesn't have to be someone we know. Making an utter stranger's day is a real joy. Cashiers in restaurants, bus and taxi drivers, street-corner news vendors—make them smile or laugh, and you'll feel great. You will make a positive human connection, however fleeting, which will make you feel good about belonging to humanity. And you'll immediately perceive yourself as being a "good egg."

Take a Well-Deserved Break. I've noticed that when I'm stressed out, I have a tendency to deny what's happening to me. I might tell myself, "Why, I can handle this stuff. I don't need any sleep. I can pull an all-nighter, if I have to. I'll be perfectly fine!" I suppose it's a form of bravado that I try to project. But what's really happening is I'm building up for a huge letdown.

I've seen the physical equivalent happen in exercise classes. If the class has been doing a very challenging workout and the instructor offers a water break, the wise students gratefully take advantage of it. The "iron horses" decline, and certainly, they are able to carry on for a while. But suddenly, they wear down just as everybody zips by them looking like Energizer bunnies. So when you start to think, "I can handle all the stress in the world—why, bring it on!" you're probably about to crack.

Do yourself a favor—take a break. If you're on the phone most of the day, get up and leave your desk. Close your eyes and think of a peaceful and beautiful place. Mentally, I visit a beach in Hawaii where I've actually jogged in utter bliss on numerous occasions. By having that memory at my command, I can take a minivacation whenever I set aside a few minutes for a break.

Take Deep, Cleansing Breaths. Consult with any yogi and you'll be informed that the average person simply doesn't know how to breathe. This sounds silly, doesn't it? Our bodies force us to breathe, so what's there to know about it?

Actually, there is quite a lot. People use various types of breathing. We're all familiar with shallow breathing because we do it most of the time. We use rejuvenation breathing to catch our breath after we have engaged in sudden exertion.

And there are cleansing breaths, which enable us to calm ourselves. I suggest you use these in two contexts. First, if you find you're in the middle of a stressful call, ask the other person to hold for a minute; then slowly take three deep breaths. I assure you that afterward your tone will sound much more pleasant and you'll feel as if you're really in control.

The second way that you can use cleansing breaths is *in advance*. Let's say a call comes in and you simply know that the person on the other end is going to sound unglued. Take three cleansing breaths before you answer the line. This will prevent you from having the wind knocked out of you. Plus, by sounding calm, you'll send a signal to the other person that everything's under control and that it's all right for that person to sound calm like you, too.

Take a Walk. Walking is truly therapeutic. You can set your own pace, and the rhythms of breathing and moving your body can be very, very soothing. Even if you're mad at somebody (including yourself), by taking your difficulty for a walk, you'll generally be able to let whatever is bothering you run its course.

Walking is also a great opportunity to hear answers to some of life's stickiest problems. As you relax to the cadence of walking, you may suddenly see things in new ways. This happens to some folks when they're jogging or even when they're on their exercise bikes.

Hit a Bag or Kick Somebody. Some overstressed folks enjoy vanquishing their emotional woes in more explosive ways. Bill, one of my friends in the neighborhood, regularly repairs to his garage to punch the boxing bag suspended from the rafters.

I enjoy the martial arts, so I actually get to hit and kick people! (Sounds brutal, but we're carefully trained to not harm each other.) I can't tell you how enjoyable it is to ventilate hostilities in controlled learning environments, which most dojos are.

Remember, the Sun Will Shine Tomorrow. *Gone with the Wind* is a classic movie for many reasons. The production is cinematically breathtaking and the story is monumental. Also, the characters are beautifully portrayed.

You may recall Scarlett O'Hara's oft-repeated line, which is one of my all-time favorites, "Tomorrow is another day!" It may sound a little trite, but it certainly is true. Every day the world is born anew, and we get a fresh chance to make the world right. No matter how besieged you feel, remember this simple fact: your problems will probably seem smaller and less nettlesome tomorrow. And you'll be a little bit older and wiser about how to address them.

Cut Yourself Some Slack. There is much evidence showing that some of life's top performers are also brutal self-critics. They just can't allow themselves to appreciate their successes without simultaneously shafting themselves with regrets.

If you ask them why they are that way, they'll respond, "Well, I'm just a perfectionist!" as if this is a positive justification. Perfectionism is a problem, not a solution. By insisting that everything be perfect, we're using a recipe for dissatisfaction and we're bound to perpetuate poor self-images.

Cut yourself some slack. Doing an excellent job is good enough. Perfection just isn't possible to attain or sustain on Earth. So don't bother yourself about it. Also, make some room for an occasional blunder or utter failure.

Real learning comes from making mistakes. When everything is running smoothly, we're not facing enough challenges. Failing is a necessary price to pay in order to make real progress.

Tell Yourself, "They, Too, Shall Pass." I read an interview with one of the best talent agents in Hollywood. He was asked whether he found it to be disconcerting dealing with tough-as-nails studio personalities. He calmly replied, "Not at all. If I'm sitting across from an idiot, I'll simply smile and tell myself, 'I'll deal with your successor.' There's *always* a successor!" Isn't that a neat philosophy? I've repeated this to myself, and it's always reliable. People move on, are fired, promoted, or simply disappear from the picture. They, too, will pass!

Don't Take It Personally

I love it when in movies, one mobster says to another as he's about to squeeze the trigger: "Nothing personal, pal. It's just business."

Business *is* business. And often when we're smack in the middle of a dispute, it's best to remember this simple fact. Fundamentally, business is about making a living. Yet many of us are tempted to muddle together our business and personal lives, and this is where we can get into emotional trouble.

When someone expresses anger at us at work, they usually criticize us while we execute our roles. For example, I might grow miffed with an airline supervisor if he refuses to honor my upgrade to first class but I can see that the front cabin is nearly empty. Do I dislike *him* as a person? Not really. What I disdain is how he's performing his business function. I'm just not getting what I want from him. Now, if I get off the plane and I'm still fuming about our little spat, then I have a problem.

How to Recognize and Reduce Defensiveness

If I'm still fuming, then I'm probably reacting defensively, which is just a technical way of saying that I consider the airline episode to be a personal affront. My internal dialogue probably sounds like this:

> *"How dare he deny me an upgrade? He has no idea of how many miles I fly every year. Why, if I wanted to, I could blackball his carrier and vow to never fly with them again. I could probably convince at least a half dozen other people in my firm to avoid that airline like the plague. Before I do, I'll write a letter to the president—that's what I'll do. I'll show that creep that he can't get away with this!"*

Clearly, I could make myself feel defensive by choosing to interpret the upgrade denial as a personal attack. Frequently, our defensive reactions can be activated by things that customers and associates say. Shirley might turn in her chair and blurt out: "Don't you ever get tired of wearing *black*?" Bill may ask you if it would be possible to lower your telephone voice to a "mild roar." Your boss may say she would really appreciate it if you could, "for once, see things my way and put in a little overtime during the weekend."

All of these statements could be interpreted as personal attacks. "I like black, you bozo," you might say, while telling her "My colors are my business!" In responding this way, you would be doing what most of us do when we feel we're being personally attacked. We defend by attacking right back.

It's akin to what we might have said to a warring sister or brother:

"You ate the last cookie, you pig!"

"Did not!"

"Did too!"

"Did not!"

"Did too, liar."

"You're the liar, not me!"

"No, you are!"

This attack-and-counterattack scenario is the signature of a defensive communication cycle. As adults, we may cloak our messages in the trappings of sophistication, but a defensive exchange remains the same no matter how young or old we are. It's almost as if the participants feel that no attack should pass by without being responded to in kind.

There are six types of messages that have a high probability of making us and others feel defensive. Any of these can launch a nettlesome cycle of attack and counterattack.

Evaluation. Name-calling is a popular way of expressing a negative evaluation of someone. In the kiddie scenario above, one sibling called the other a "little pig" and then a "liar." These accusations are fighting words, and it's completely foreseeable that a spat will result from their use.

Sometimes name-calling is more subtle because it is implicit. When the boss asked if an employee could work overtime "for once," she might really have been saying that the employee wasn't a team player or was selfish for wanting to keep her weekends to herself.

The coworker who commented about her colleague always wearing black may have been saying that she found it tiresome, boring, or even outright ugly. She may have been saying that her colleague was unfashionable or even tasteless. Unquestionably, her comment was negative, despite the fact that she didn't use a specific adjective to describe her feelings about her colleague's wardrobe selections.

Control. When someone tries to control us, it can make us feel weak and powerless. Controlling comments can take several forms.

In the office situation, one person asked another if he could lower his telephone voice to a mild roar. Obviously, this is an overt attempt to control someone else's behavior. A person accused of miscommunicating in this way might think: "My voice isn't loud. Anyway, that's how I always talk, so why doesn't he mind his own business?" Or, the defensive person might decide to retaliate. "I'll show him. I'll whisper, and customers won't be able to hear me. They'll ask me why I'm whispering and I'll tell them that my associate said I was too loud. That'll embarrass him, all right!"

Strategy. When you were a kid, do you remember asking a friend about something and then hearing him or her snicker: "Well, that's for me to know, and for you to find out"?

This is the mood of strategic messages. When people act strategically, they're trying to prevent us from finding out what we want to know. For example, I mentioned to a friend that I was going to increase my professional speaking dates. She immediately said, "I know someone who books speakers." I said, "That's great. What's her name?" Instantly, my once-glib pal clammed up and muttered, "Well, it's just someone I ran into once." She didn't want me to get in touch with the person directly. She may have been trying to "broker" any deal that I might strike with her contact. Possibly, she was envious of the fact that

I was making rapid progress in my career, while hers was stalled. No matter what her motivation was, I determined that she definitely was being strategic with me.

So how did I respond? I noted her reaction and let it pass for the time being. But I also made a mental note that she really wasn't the unselfish pal I had hoped she would be. In other words, I determined that I had to be a little strategic around her, as well.

Again, one defensive message begets another.

Neutrality. I was having a conversation with a client in which I was expressing a lot of enthusiasm for a project we were working on. Instead of mirroring my attitude, she simply dryly approved of the project. I asked her what she thought, and she deadpanned: "That'll work."

This neutral phrase seemed completely inappropriate to the tenor of our discussion to that point. What I discovered later was the fact that she had attended a seminar that urged participants to delete positives and negatives from their vocabularies. So, instead of responding with, "That's great," or even "Very good," she was trained to simply communicate in unemotional, functional terms. I could have said anything to her, like "Gee, we won the lottery!" and I probably would have evoked the same lackluster, neutral reply.

You can imagine how the same sort of flat response might upset a customer. Imagine that you're a customer worried about the possibility you won't receive a critical shipment. You phone your vendor, only to get this sort of neutral reception:

"Acme Baskets, this is Trudy."

"Hi, Trudy. I have a real problem. I ordered a dozen baskets which I need to get today, or I'm dead meat, if you know what I mean. Can you see where it is?"

"What's your account number, please?"

"A-32216."

"One moment."

"Gee, I hope you can track it."

"One moment. No, I don't see it on my screen. It's not in the system."

"Oh, my gosh. What'll I do?"

"Hold on. I'll check our hard copies."

If you got a sinking feeling as you read this exchange, then I got my point across. Neutrality makes us feel as if we're being left out in the cold.

To complicate matters, many people actually try to sound neutral, mistakenly believing that this helps them to come across as more professional. Unfortunately, what they regard as professional simply sounds detached and unconcerned to customers.

Superiority. There are many services we can buy on the open market where suppliers have superior know-how. Their know-how is central to their value. Most of us wouldn't bother visiting attorneys, architects, and other professionals but for the fact that they know important facts and procedures we don't know.

At the same time, we can feel somewhat vulnerable because of this knowledge gap. We don't want others to lord it over us when they refer to their expertise or to our amateurishness. For instance, I wouldn't appreciate it if my physician declared: "Look, Gary, I didn't spend twelve years becoming a doctor to hear you tell me what's wrong with you!" This sort of superiority really has no place in a constructive dialogue, yet as you know, it creeps into many conversations. And any of us can be guilty of slipping into a mode of superiority.

For example, I conduct customer service and service management seminars across the country. During my introduction and overview portion I mention the process I've undertaken to scientifically validate a number of new procedures. I have noticed that the more time I spend with this sort of background, the more testy my attendees become. It's as if they're saying to themselves, "Yeah, we know you're smart. Now get to the stuff that really matters!" So I've curtailed the long-winded preliminaries, because instead of enhancing credibility and the likelihood that my information will be used, it backfires.

Certainty. In the same seminars, I might have occasionally said: "This technique really works. I guarantee if you say this, you'll get the result you want." Believe it or not, even this statement could be taken defensively. We don't want to seem so self-assured, so cocky, and so arrogant that we come across as saying: "I am absolutely, 100 percent right about this."

Guess what people want to do when we seem to know it all? That's right, they want to prove us wrong. In fact, they'll interrupt their lives and commit themselves to the single-minded mission of unpuffing our puffery. We're certain we're right and they're certain we're wrong!

It's another reminder of what happens when we purposely or mistakenly use defensive messages. Our listeners will use them right back at us.

Evaluate people by calling them bad names, and they'll hurl names back at you. Try to control people, and they'll control you. Cleverly conceal something from them and they'll cleverly withhold information from you. Sound cold and neutral and you'll chill your relationship. Act in a superior way, and they'll show you how superior they are. And, as we just saw, they'll puncture your balloon of certainty with their own certain convictions that you must be wrong.

Life May Not Be Fair, but Sooner or Later, Justice Will Be Served

It's easy to "awfulize" about matters that don't go our way. Many people blurt out, "It's just not fair." They've been brought up to believe that life operates with some sense of equity, at least in the short run.

I'm not going to tell you the opposite—that life is unfair. Actually, it is both fair and unfair. The teenage rock star, who has never known anything but luxury, cuts a recording that soars to the top of the charts. Millions of dollars are lavished upon him, and he never has to punch a time clock or answer to a boss. Is that fair? In a sense, no, it isn't fair. The coal miner labors longer and harder and faces disability and death every day. The teenager's greatest trauma may be the appearance of a pimple.

Yet in another sense, if the rocker has composed or performed a tune that gives millions of folks such pleasure that they buy the recording, then he has provided a service that isn't trifling. And he should share in the bounty that he has created.

Life still may put that young person through his paces. What if his fame suddenly ends, and nobody wants to hear his music or watch him perform? Isn't that a form of psychic punishment? Possibly, he could be pained every day because he thinks his good fortune should return just as easily as it first appeared. Therefore, he waits for luck to intervene, while his circumstances grow more desperate and his slide descends lower.

So in the short run life may be grossly unfair. But in the fullness of time, things balance out. A go-go growth company's employee who has no time to speak to you, because he's too busy "carrying barrels filled with money to the bank," could be singing a different tune when the economy turns or competitors suddenly spring forth.

I actually had a sales prospect tell me that he wasn't interested in my consulting services because he was wheeling big money to his local financial institution. Later, I heard that his franchiser bought him out, simply to get him out of its hair and system.

Once, I was competing for a consulting contract against a division of a Fortune 500 company. Its salesperson pulled an interesting stunt. He knew I was his rival and that I intended to personally do the work if I won the contract. Typically, his company distributed a large assignment among several trainers, who would simultaneously perform the job.

So playing to the fear of putting all of one's eggs into a single basket, my adversary challenged the prospect with this outrageous appeal: "What would happen if Goodman died during the performance of the contract?" Believe it or not, this question was sufficient to scare the buyer, who revealed the statement to me some time later.

I didn't die—as I'm sure you gathered—but my competitor's company did! It was sold off within a few years, and subsequently it was sold again. Moreover, the buyer's company faced the same sort of demise as it was put on the sales block during the same period.

But the greatest comeuppance came later. My competitors actually hired *me* to train their national field sales force and to create an inside selling program! So let me ask you: Is there justice in the world?

I think so. Once you recognize that there is truth in the phrase, "They'll get theirs," you'll be able to comfort yourself, come what may.

You don't have to be the instrument of retribution. It will come in its own time. Just make it a point to tune in later. The story always changes.

Pack the Profit into the Next Deal

When I was in the car-leasing business right after college, I had an opportunity to negotiate a contract with a true corporate shark. This CEO ground me to bits, and then, after I had acquired a car for him, he refused delivery because he felt the interior color wasn't exactly as it appeared on the color chip.

I conferred with my management, and they advised me to find him another car that was a perfect fit in terms of his color preference. The car we found wasn't nearly as loaded with extra features as the model he refused, but he accepted delivery anyway.

It turned out that we were able to transform a terrible deal into a very good one, because we were able to realize a bigger profit from the second car. The client paid the same price, but he got much less of a car for the money. He didn't know it, but we did. What goes around, comes around, right?

Don't Be Afraid to Flash Some Assertiveness

I hope you're getting the idea that there are several ways to manage conflict and to remain tranquil at the same time. Many of these methods, so far, have dealt with techniques for quelling our negative feelings as they arise.

But in this section, I want to point out that it can pay off to show some assertiveness, because it can literally shock people into treating you with respect, and it may induce them to retreat from the hostile positions they've taken.

For instance, I was set to deliver a seminar before a university continuing education audience, when my contact suddenly wanted to slant our financial arrangements more in his favor. We were having coffee about an hour before the program was scheduled to begin, when he broke this disquieting news to me.

I had to quickly make a decision. Do I cave in to his demand for a reshuffling of the economic deck and become upset as I deliver my lecture, or do I protest and possibly have to cancel the program?

I didn't like the alternatives, but I had to act. I told him, "I believe in the sanctity of contracts, and one party shouldn't decide to change it after he has made a commitment." With my steely glare piercing him, he knew I meant business. Clearing his throat, he said that he had misunderstood our agreement, but he would uphold his end of it anyway.

The program came off without a glitch. Moreover, he and I had very smooth dealings for many years afterward. Both of us spoke our minds, and we got along in an atmosphere of friendliness and mutual respect.

I look back upon my showing of assertiveness as an essential event that set the proper boundaries for our dealings. Occasionally, you'll find that you need to do likewise, despite the fact that it may appear, at least in the short run, that you're adding fuel to a fire.

Be Like Water

Water is one of the strongest as well as one of the weakest of nature's elements. If it's formed into a tidal wave, it can batter civilizations. When it flows with less power, it can quietly circumvent any object in its way. Water can't be cut or bruised. It can't be broken or chipped. When someone comes at you with great emotional force, instead of becoming a wall or a hammer, try to become like water.

Don't give your adversary anything to resist. One way to do this is to partially agree with the person. Let's say that a customer tells you: "I'm really pissed off. Your delivery was late, so I had to go over to my competitor and buy enough hats, at retail prices, just to satisfy my customers and make my deadlines. You cost me a lot of money, and I expect to be compensated for this!"

"Well you make perfect sense," you can respond, but then continue, "Though we see the situation differently." What are you doing with this phrase? You're agreeing, but then disagreeing.

You might suspect that this mixed message is going to come across as confusing or as self-canceling. However, it will work. Here's the reason: When customers are angry, they need an emotional satisfaction along with a concrete, real-world resolution of the matter. By telling an angry person, "You make perfect sense," you're authenticating his or her logic; you're telling that person that he or she is OK as a person and not crazy to be upset. But immediately after saying this, you also tell that person implicitly that because you have a different take on the matter you're going to offer a different resolution than the one he or she is trying to impose upon you.

Being like water isn't our natural tendency in a situation such as this one. Commonly, we stiffen our resolve to be like rocks, unbending and unyielding. When we react this way, we simply induce our adversaries to adopt a harder line. This cycle leads to greater misunderstandings and more losses, all around.

In the next chapter, I'll provide you with several transition phrases that will give you additional ways to disagree while agreeing. To be waterlike.

Develop Some Outside Interests

I had the good fortune to have worked my way through college and graduate school. In a sense I was lucky that my education wasn't paid for by anyone other than myself. This may sound contrary to common sense, but the experience was great for this reason. Because I was always doing two major things at once—being a student and being employed—I found that at least one activity was usually going well, even as the other seemed to be lagging behind. I was getting raises and promotions despite having to face the gloom of midterm and final exams at school. And when I earned an A on an assignment, it felt like money in the bank, even if my actual bank balance was diminishing.

By engaging in two activities, I didn't take either of them too seriously. I always enjoyed going to school after work, because it seemed like such a privilege, and working was simply a great experience, as well.

Unfortunately, as adults we can grow narrower—so narrow that our careers become the sum total of our lives. Don't let this happen to you. Take a class at a local school, or join a community theater group, or check out a martial arts or dancing studio where you can immerse yourself, and at least temporarily forget about the job and its stresses.

Outlaw Self-Downing

Many of us carry around an internal critic who says things like: "You really blew it," and "Gee, this is going to screw up, buddy." This critic is like a very gloomy prophet who predicts disaster at every turn.

I'm not sure we can ever completely silence this backseat driver, but we can rebut him with positive statements. "Even if I blew it, I'm going to be OK, and make the most of the situation," we should counter. And we can assure ourselves, "Even if this does screw up, so what—the world will keep turning." In other words, if a critic inhabits our consciousness, it shouldn't get all of the limelight. Put a friend in there, who can supplant the negatives with positives.

It's one thing for our associates, our customers, and our peers to gang up on us. By all means, don't jump into the fray and pile on yourself!

The Best Revenge Is in Learning

Almost every experience gives us a second chance, if we're wise enough to learn from it. To ensure that we learn, I've crafted an eight-point reminder list that spells the word L-E-A-R-N-I-N-G.

Let the negative event or conflict fully develop in your mind. Don't repress it or downplay it, as will be your initial impulse. You'll probably find that the worst thing that can happen isn't so awful.

Evaluate exactly what is happening. Try to describe it dispassionately, as a third-person observer would do. This will make it appear objective and much more manageable.

Ask yourself what learning points may be disguised in this event. Many entrepreneurs report that they lose small fortunes and find themselves repeatedly broke before having their final financial breakthroughs. Their secret is knowing that they can correct nearly any flaw or inadequacy, provided they know what lessons their experiences have in store for them.

Resolve to transform every defeat into a victory and to change ashes into gold dust. When you're constantly poised to find the silver lining, you'll take more noble risks, because you'll count on yourself to mine the best from every situation.

Negate negative thinking. Don't allow yourself to take on other people's morose and limited visions of what is possible or

impossible. They aren't you, and they don't have your gift for
recovery or for applying imagination to challenging situations.

Immerse yourself in the wonders of events. Isn't it interesting that
life is throwing such challenges your way at this very moment?
It must think you can handle them, so who are you to disagree? You've heard the expression, "If you want to get something done, just ask a busy person to do it." The logic is that
busy people are people who know how to get things done. People who face problems and conflict are usually endowed with
the capacity to solve their difficulties. Isn't that wondrous?

Note all of your conflicts and stresses in a log. Update it daily.
Refer to it as time passes; it is a testimony to your capability
to overcome huge obstacles. It will be an inspiration to you,
I'm sure.

Go beyond the conflict in your mind. Imagine the dust settling
and the sun shining through. Calamities end, sooner or later,
and we can accelerate their resolutions by imagining the circumstances that will follow. So prepare to prevail over your
disappointments, setbacks, and tensions, because you will!

Resolve to Stay Positive in Outlook, Come What May

Whenever I'm about to plunge into negativity, I try to follow these
seven suggestions. They've worked for my clients and I hope they'll
serve you well:

1. Tell yourself, "Every day, in every way, I'm getting better and better." This statement is a great antidote to the toxins we feed ourselves,
especially as we age. Typically, we tell ourselves that we're getting
worse physically, intellectually, and attitudinally.

By saying, "I'm getting better and better," we remind ourselves that
we are improving and that our experiences, including adversarial ones,
are strengthening us. I assure you that you'll immediately feel an
improvement in your outlook after you repeat that helpful line, which
was first coined by psychologist Emile Coue several years ago.

2. Remember how far you've come in order to be at your present level of effectiveness. It's easy to forget that we came into this world without a handbook or operating instructions. We've had to learn nearly everything simply to survive. And the skills you currently have are the consequences of a tremendous amount of trial and error as well as explicit instruction from others.

So if you're facing difficulties, it isn't for the first time. You've met the challenges in the past, and you'll do it again.

3. Remember others who haven't made it to your level. We know that the race doesn't always go to the swift. Take a moment to remember those colleagues and buddies in various situations who didn't make it through the ordeals that you faced together.

Recently, my martial arts *sensei* reminded me of my entering class at the Institute. About half quit the training or were deemed inappropriate for receiving further instruction—yet I'm still around. By bringing this to my attention, my *sensei* was reminding me that I have the right stuff to succeed. When viewed this way, I can see my difficulties as temporary—as stepping stones instead of stumbling blocks.

4. Do something nice for yourself. Take yourself out to a movie or for a drive into the country or by the sea. Buy yourself a trinket. Or just play hooky for an hour or two and escape to your nearest public library, where you can become blissfully lost in the stacks.

When we're stressed out, one of the last things we consider doing is rewarding ourselves, but this may be just what we need. It's a way of taking care of ourselves, and we shouldn't always have to look to other people to do it for us.

5. If you think rewarding yourself is a little too self-indulgent, then turn your benevolence in the direction of other people. Do something kind and unexpected for the less fortunate. This can take any form, from donating money to giving your time. My projects usually center around education, so I find myself helping out the schools I've attended, or I'll donate books to libraries.

These endeavors aren't completely selfless. In fact, I get a tremendous return from them inasmuch as they help me to get outside of myself, at least temporarily. And when I do, I find that I literally forget about my own stresses and difficulties.

6. Count your blessings. This may seem to be a corny suggestion, but it works for me. I can feel utterly besieged by deadlines and by the impact of negative personalities, but when I stop to consider my situation, it sparkles when compared to the circumstances many other people face. At least I have the physical and mental wherewithal to solve my difficulties. If I have made my bed, so to speak, I can usually remake it.

7. Don't be afraid to ask for help. Many of the suggestions offered in this chapter you can implement completely by yourself. But there are occasions when your own resources won't be enough.

You may find that you feel stuck and completely depleted of motivation. In a word, you may be depressed. If it doesn't pass rather quickly, and your feelings of gloom simply grow more dire, please reach out to others for help.

The National Institute of Mental Health offers a checklist on the Internet that can help you to see if you may be depressed. The website address is: www.nimh.nih.gov. You can also phone your local hospital or free clinic to receive a referral to a therapist who can shepherd you through your difficulties.

You don't have to go it alone. (This is especially important for men to know. We're famous for refusing to ask for help when we're lost.)

Summary

This chapter has given you a psychological framework for preventing and managing conflict. You've learned how to control your own reactions to negative events. The next chapter will show you some of the best ways to construct messages that will enable you to communicate your way through the most challenging business situations.

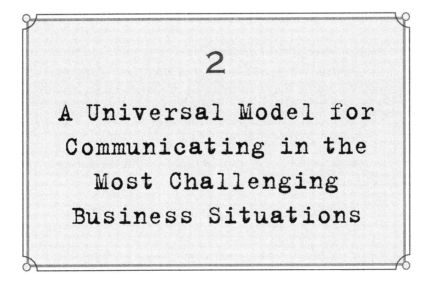

2

A Universal Model for Communicating in the Most Challenging Business Situations

Do you ever feel tongue-tied or have difficulty organizing what you're going to say during stressful conversations?

Would you like a method for calming customers down before having to explain other things to them?

Do you ever feel that your apologies aren't being received very well?

Do you ever feel it's difficult to come across as being professional and friendly at the same time?

When customers have difficulties with your products, policies, or personnel, would you like to have a neat way of compensating them for their troubles?

Do customers ever feel that you're not acting sincerely or completely honestly with them?

Are you concerned that if you admit blame, it might encourage further anger in customers, and even promote lawsuits?

Would you like some solid ways to express empathy, apart from saying, "I'm sorry"?

Would you like a method for making your point in a firm way, without raising your voice?

Would you like to have some short but pleasant phrases that will enable you to assert control over a conversation?

IN THIS CHAPTER, you'll learn: to address people's emotions first, as you handle tough conversations; the fine art of apologizing; the differences between good manners and sincerity; how to seem professional, but friendly; how to compensate people for their troubles; how to use your voice tones to reinforce your points; how to avoid making legal admissions that can land you in court; how to sound empathic, with and without saying, "I'm sorry"; how to use the three-part PEP format to organize your ideas on the spot; how to improvise in a heartbeat; how to be super-persuasive by calmly "proving opposites"; how to keep cool and avoid shouting; and how to use transition phrases to assert gentle but firm control over conversations.

$$*\qquad*\qquad*\qquad*\qquad*\qquad*\qquad*$$

Have you ever stopped to admire those silver-tongued devils who seem to have an answer for every question and the perfect patter for all occasions? Perhaps, thinking that their abilities sprouted from genius, you may have felt that you could never match them.

Not so. Many of the most effective communicators use proven methods to format their talks. Often, these methods are unknown to them, and consequently, they use them unconsciously. I'm going to share with you a universal model that emulates what articulate people do to communicate effectively in the most challenging business situations. This way, you can start sounding like a genius without further delay.

You'll have PEP (point, evidence, point) at hand. It's a nifty and nimble organizational skeleton upon which you can construct the best responses on the spot to any challenge. Through its three simple steps, you'll gain the capability of explaining the most peculiar rules and regulations in reasonable ways. It will help you to develop a knack for explaining your way out of thorny business situations. Instead of feeling like a bull in a china shop, you'll come across with poise and composure.

Two agendas operate simultaneously in challenging situations. The first agenda is usually an emotional one. People are uptight because they know or at least suspect that something is wrong. So, they prepare themselves for disaster and brace to hear the worst. Quite frequently, they're mentally blaming us for their plight, while chastising themselves for interacting with us. So by the time we actually sit down to talk or call them on the phone, they're like loaded revolvers, ready to blow us away at the least provocation.

The second agenda is informational. It relates to the official topic under discussion. For instance, if we are late in delivering a shipment, this agenda will explain why we're running late and try to predict when the expected items will arrive.

As you might guess, there is a commonly accepted order in which we should address these agendas. The general rule is to address the emotional one first, and the informational one second.

So we might say the following:

"Hello, Mary? This is Gary Goodman. I'm sorry, but I want you to know that our shipment is running a few hours late. I've been in touch with the driver and he has promised that it will definitely be there by four o'clock, OK? Again, I'm sorry for any inconvenience, and thank you for your business. Bye."

What if we reversed the order, and announced the informational component first, while delaying the emotional part? How would this change affect the meaning the customer would get?

"Hello, Mary? This is Gary Goodman. Our shipment is running a few hours late. I've been in touch with the driver and he has promised that it will definitely be there by four o'clock, OK? Sorry. Bye."

By addressing the emotions explicitly, we accomplish many things. The next section will discuss the art of apologizing. Then I'll present the best methods for organizing the content of your sensitive communications.

Mastering the Fine Art of the Apology

"But I'm not sorry!" Jill blurted out to her fellow seminar participants at the University of Toledo.

Silence swept over the group, followed by waves of laughter. No one could quite believe that a worker who was being paid to attend a seminar on customer service would admit to being unsympathetic to clients.

"What do you mean?" I responded. "You're not sorry about what?"

"I'm not sorry that the customer is angry. Where I work, it's usually the shipping department's fault that someone's mad at us!"

"You've got that right!" someone sympathized from a few seats over.

As the seminar leader, I needed to clarify her position. "So are you saying if you haven't been the primary *cause* of the customer's anger, you shouldn't have to apologize?"

"Exactly," she barked back.

"Well, that's an interesting viewpoint," I said, as I tried to assimilate the significance of what she was saying. Then it hit me. "But you're in customer service, right? If you don't apologize, who will?"

"That's not my problem," she shot back with steely self-righteousness.

However radical it may seem, Jill articulated a feeling that many businesspeople foster, but few express. They feel that:

- They shouldn't have to apologize for the mistakes of their associates or for events that they didn't personally set into motion.
- If they do apologize in such circumstances, they would be acting insincerely.
- Employers shouldn't place them in such uncomfortable situations to begin with.

"I Think I *Deserve* an Apology!"

Of course, the impulse to avoid apologizing flies in the face of customer expectations. Most of us, as consumers and as buyers in business situations, expect to hear apologies. Have you ever heard the expression: "I think I deserve an apology"?

For the mistreated, an apology is a perceived entitlement. It is also a form of emotional compensation. A proper apology explicitly acknowledges that another party has been put through discomfort or has experienced an otherwise uncompensated loss. By showing sensitivity, we pay people for their troubles.

Moreover, a prompt apology tends to have preventive value—it dissuades a disgruntled person from increasing his or her anger. When we apologize quickly, we immediately send a message that says we realize that we've transgressed, and we will be vigilant to avoid further problems.

On the other hand, if we delay in issuing an apology, we can seem callous and unconcerned for the other party's welfare. This promotes a two-part conflict: first we screwed up, and then we didn't even care about the fact that we did so. This leaves a "victim" in the position of regretting the original decision to do business with us.

Half-Hearted Apologies Don't Go Far Enough

It's generally accepted that the more effusive the apology, the more soothing it will be to the listener. By showing a proper quantum of contrition, we'll actually set into motion a very productive dynamic. Sufferers will see that we're feeling vicarious pain, and they'll empathize with us. At that moment, both parties will identify with each other's plight, and a cleansing of negative emotions will often result.

In everyday terms, we refer to this process of a mutual purgation of the emotions as *venting* or *clearing the air*. When this occurs, people let go of their hostile feelings and seldom seek retribution. Consequently, apologies serve the mighty purpose of precluding hostilities from being carried over into future transactions.

The test of a good apology is that it induces the other party to promptly and wholeheartedly forgive us. If people don't say the equivalent of, "That's OK," or "It isn't your fault," or "Don't worry about it—I'll be OK," then our apologies have been less than completely effective.

By the same token, if we only issue half-hearted apologies, we allow the embers of hostility to burn, and they'll burn for quite a while. Let's say we screw up again, within short order. The person who half forgave us will really flare up the second time around, causing irreparable harm to our relationship.

Good Manners Shouldn't Be Confused with Sincerity

Noted management consultant and author Peter Drucker has observed, in many seminars I have taken from him at Claremont Graduate University, that many young people like Jill confuse good manners with acting insincerely. They believe they actually must *feel* contrite in order to apologize to clients and fellow businesspeople.

Drucker emphatically points out that "Manners have nothing to do with sincerity. All they are is lubricating oil." Drucker says that good manners merely help people to interact with less friction. In a sense, they're like rules of the road, which keep us from plowing our cars into each other. He points out that without manners, "there would be chaos."

Then Again, Jill Made a Good Point

Jill did make a point—at least by implication—that is worth discussing. She said she didn't feel she should have to apologize for someone else's blunder. I side with Drucker and think she should soothe her customers more and not confuse her actions with sincerity or insincerity.

At the same time, she raises an interesting possibility. In her case, is there any reason the shipping manager shouldn't also apologize for a major customer mishap? It couldn't hurt, and it might actually make the shipping function more accountable.

A number of years ago, I started noticing that when I bought certain clothes, little messages were found in the pockets. Generally, they were inscribed with a little phrase such as "Inspected by 51." The more customer-focused firms personalized their messages—"Inspected by Sarah."

What do you think happens to quality control in such manufacturing companies? That's right—it improves, because accountability and ownership of results are introduced into the product-making process.

Jill's notion could certainly improve the quality of everyone's work if offenders had to personally apologize for their mistakes. This wouldn't be done, one hopes, in a punitive atmosphere where perpetrators would feel stigmatized. Nonetheless, having to come forward out of obscurity or anonymity should impel them to do their future work with much greater diligence.

Misplaced Professionalism: An Obstacle to Building Positive Relationships

Apologies are actually useful for everybody. Yet Jill isn't alone in not wanting to issue them. I've run into numerous people who believe that showing remorse and expressing contrition are signs of weakness, which reflect a degree of unprofessionalism.

How do they arrive at this conclusion? They believe that professionalism is a valuable characteristic for them to manifest. They tacitly define *professionalism* as doing one's duty without injecting one's private self into the matter. Therefore, they avoid showing emotions or expressing opinions about their work. You might think of these folks as you would the character Arnold Schwarzenegger played in the movie, *The Terminator*. You may recall that he was a cyborg with one purpose: to track down and terminate the character played by actress Linda Hamilton. He didn't laugh or show emotion. He simply did his job until it was done.

Unfortunately, people who behave like the Terminator actually create more harm than good. Instead of coming across as fair and objective (which they think they are) they appear to most people as being uncaring and callous. They would do everyone a favor by practicing their apologies!

Putting Money Where Our Mouths Are

What do airlines do when they oversell a flight and they have to turn away passengers at the gate? They pay the stranded for their trouble, in money, free tickets, or frequent-flier miles.

This is a very clear and well-received method of expressing an apology to someone who has been inconvenienced. For example, one of my clients mentioned that he found one of my audiocassettes to be lower in sound quality than the rest of the set. Instead of putting him through the bother of packaging and shipping the tape back to me, I apologized and told him to keep it as a backup. Moreover, I sent him a replacement tape along with a free autographed book for his troubles. A few short months later, when I produced a new video series, the same client was the very first to place an order. Obviously, he felt he would be treated well. He was also confident that I would stand behind my products.

By giving people something extra, we acknowledge that we take responsibility for our actions; that is, we know people experience actual costs when we inconvenience them. Also, we show that we're ready, willing, and committed to help defray some of these costs because we are sincere and value our relationships.

Here is an example of this kind of apology:

> "We're really sorry we've inconvenienced you, and we want to show you that we value your business (our relationship). So we'll credit your account for the full purchase price of the item, and we'll also send you a free gift certificate. May we do that for you?

> "It'll be our pleasure, and thank you for doing business with us!"

Which Is Better: "I'm Sorry" or "We're Sorry"?

Would Jill have felt a little better about saying "We're sorry," instead of "I'm sorry"? And would it have been equally effective in soothing the listener?

We is an institutional term, isn't it? It represents a collective, instead of an individual sentiment. There are lots of jokes about doctors and nurses who visit hospitalized patients and inquire: "How are *we* today?"

"I'm OK Doc, but you look terrible!" In other words, the word *we* can seem to create pseudointimacy, instead of the real thing. Consequently, it can backfire and miscommunicate. The person might think, "That person doesn't really care about *me* as an individual." "How are you feeling this morning?" sounds much more genuine.

But take a look at the previous example of an apology.

I used *we* when I had the rep offer a free gift certificate to the inconvenienced customer. Why would I do that if *we* sounds more institutional? When giving away money, or its equivalent, I think making the person feel like the entire company or organization is involved serves a proper purpose. Partly, this is to protect the rep. We don't want customers to think that the rep has sole discretion as to whether and when to bestow gratuities of this magnitude. If clients thought reps could cut their own deals, and in effect, choose to give away money, then requests for such treatment could quickly multiply.

Yet in other situations, saying "I'm sorry" would be much more appropriate. Let's say you forgot to call someone back despite having made an explicit promise to do so. This memory lapse wasn't made by a huge bureaucracy, but by a solitary individual. So saying, "I blew it, and I'm really sorry," would be received much better than an apology from collective lips, "We try to return all of our calls, but sometimes we can't!" By comparison, this sounds very lame, doesn't it?

Let Your Apology Sink In

The sincerity of our apology often is indicated by how we express it, as much if not more than the words we employ. So it makes sense to orchestrate our *tones* in order to sound as sincere as we really are.

This may seem like an incongruity, like "planned spontaneity," but it isn't. Here's the reason we have to *try* to sound sincere. Left to our own "default settings" with which we speak, we normally sound *insincere* unless we fight against this impulse. The reason has to do with our desire to conserve energy. When we talk, we use words and phrases that we've used many times before. So in a sense, much of what we say has been scripted into pat phrases and clichés.

"Gee, I'm sorry about that," may be a phrase we would summon up if we bump into someone who enters a door just as we are exiting.

How would we utter this line? It would sound reflexive or automatic, and therefore, if the collision seemed less than severe, our tones might be somewhat flat. Graphing the phrase, it might look like this:

"Gee! I'm sorry about that . . ."

If the other person slipped and fell in a heap, our phrase might sound like this:

"Gee!

    I'm

        sorry

            about

                that . . ."

In other words, our tones would descend, as if we were moving down a melodic flight of stairs. The graver the situation, the farther down we dig—tonally. We actually let our genuine concern sink in. This makes us and our sentiments much more effective.

To sound like utter airheads, all we have to do is reverse the pattern and "ask" the phrase, with an ascending voice pattern, instead of uttering it as a declarative sentence:

                that . . ."

            about

        sorry

    I'm

"Gee!

This last rendering makes us sound befuddled by what happened. It also makes the apology seem halfhearted, as if we're not convinced we should even apologize for what happened.

As an experiment, I suggest you read these three phrases with the intonations that I've graphed for you. You should actually *feel* the differences in meaning that the respective versions arouse. This exercise dramatically demonstrates the power of voice tones to determine meaning.

Looking back upon the three tone patterns provided, which of these would evoke the most forgiveness from another person? If you said the middle one, you're absolutely right. When we want to communicate contrition or convey the idea that we're grieving or at least that we're apologetic, our tones should sound somber, which is like striking the leftward keys of a piano in descending order. On the other hand, when we want to come across as perky and bright, our tones normally rise.

We can also use the rate at which we speak to reinforce our point. For instance, if we rapidly scoot through the phrase, "Gee, I'm sorry about that," we would probably sound less than genuine. If, however, we utter the identical phrase slowly, our words will much more likely ring true.

As you know, placing emphasis upon certain words has a big impact upon meaning as well. Here's another experiment for you. Emphasize a different word with each vocalization of this phrase.

- *"**Gee**, I'm sorry about that . . ."*
- *"Gee, **I'm** sorry about that . . ."*
- *"Gee, I'm **sorry** about that . . ."*
- *"Gee, I'm sorry **about** that . . ."*
- *"Gee, I'm sorry about **that** . . ."*

Which version would be most comforting to the listener? The first one, by emphasizing *Gee*, tends to make you sound somewhat surprised by what happened. There is also a sense of spontaneity about *Gee*. When we say this after bumping into someone, it makes the event sound like an accident—an innocent mistake whereby we intended no harm. So the first emphasis pattern is useful.

By punching out the word *I'm*, what do we accomplish? I think it makes us sound as if we're taking responsibility for what occurred. It's like owning up to the mishap by saying, "Sorry, my mistake."

It only follows that if we emphasize the word *sorry*, we dramatize the fact that we feel a significant amount of empathy for the other person. This is certainly a desirable message to convey.

By making *about* stand out, there seems to be a disconnection between our emphasis and our words. It would probably make us sound insincere and somewhat out to lunch.

If we emphasize the word *that*, it sounds sarcastic, which is the last tone in the world we want to express. With a sarcastic tone we actually repudiate what our words typically mean. We're saying, "Don't believe my words—believe the opposite!"

Try to become increasingly aware of how you come across when you speak so you'll be able to send the exact message you want, through words as well as through the effective use of your voice.

Can Apologizing Get You into Legal Trouble?

We live in a litigious society where many folks are overeager to slap lawsuits upon any and all who may offend them in any way. We shouldn't ignore this sad fact of life, because we don't want to apologize our way into a courtroom.

How could this happen? Let's say someone was physically injured as a result of doing business with your company. Walking up to the box office at your theater, that person slipped and fell on a slick surface, and sprained an ankle. Of course, if you were there, you would want to offer that person assistance and find out how severely he or she was injured. But you wouldn't want to blurt out, "Gee, I'm so sorry. I knew someone would fall on this slick cement sooner or later!"

In a legal sense, this blurt could constitute what is called an admission. It says, "We're at fault here!" and it can be very problematic when introduced into testimony. By showing that you or your company knowingly harbored a hazardous condition, it could also ratchet up the amount of damages that a plaintiff could be awarded.

You can still show empathy by saying, "We're going to do everything we can to help you. Is there anyone I can call for you, who might want to be here as we get you the proper attention?" If you concentrate on making the person feel as comfortable as possible while waiting for medical help, you'll be doing the best of all possible things. But whatever you do, don't assign or accept blame. It's not relevant, nor is it really helpful to anyone.

The Empathic Nonapology

How can we defuse a potentially volatile encounter without issuing an apology or accepting blame? Can we provide the Jills of the world with a strategy that avoids saying "I blew it," or "I had nothing to do with this"?

I think we can. What we need to do is practice forming empathic messages. Empathy is an emotion we feel when we identify with the plight of another person. To a degree, we share their pain either because we have suffered as they are suffering, or we can imagine ourselves in their shoes.

Empathy is one of the greatest human emotions. The ability to put ourselves into other people's places, at least temporarily, is the well-spring from which drama and other arts gain their power over us. If we couldn't vicariously experience what others have gone through or are going through, it would be useless to pick up a newspaper or a novel. In fact, we applaud those artists who can craft their symbols so they make us feel our humanity—our basic and enduring link with other people.

When we find ourselves in difficult communication situations, we, too, can function artistically. Instead of making a person feel what we feel, we're trying to tell them we feel something similar to what they feel. Conveying this sentiment well can create a strong sense of identification and a sense of trust in the other person. These senses are pivotal in formulating lasting and effective interpersonal relationships.

So how do we do it? What messages can we formulate to convey our empathy? There are several that will work.

"I've Been in Your Shoes."

A good way to express empathy is to tell the person that we ourselves have been in his or her situation. After I was hit by a car while crossing the street, I was amazed by the number of people who told me they had been injured in similar circumstances. Many told me they were innocently pedaling their bikes when suddenly they were blind-sided. I have to say it was comforting to know that others had experienced what I was going through.

Occasionally, we blame ourselves for the mishaps that befall us. So when a listener empathizes by saying he or she has been in our situation, it makes us feel that we aren't utter oddities or hapless bozos. That's nice to know.

Of course, if we go too far with this type of message it could boomerang. For example, it wouldn't be very soothing if someone said to me, "You think your accident was bad? Well, I was laid up in the hospital for three weeks!" This comment would one-up me, and by doing so it trivializes my pain, instead of truly empathizing with it.

Predict a Positive Outcome

Another way to show empathy is to predict a positive ending to the unfolding drama. If you're conducting an exit interview with someone who has been laid off by your company, you would be helpful to convey the hope that something better will come along for that person in the near future. This implicitly taps into the well-accepted adage "Out of bad comes good."

The paramedics who treated me at the scene of my accident examined me and, after moving my limbs, concluded, "You're lucky that there's movement in your hands and feet. You're cut up, but you're going to be all right." Despite the fact that I was in pain when I heard these words, I felt relieved to hear that the worst was nearly over. I say "nearly" because the same paramedics predicted I would really start to feel the magnitude of my wounds later, after I was stitched up at the hospital.

Sure enough, after I was released later that evening, I felt the pain had quadrupled. Nonetheless, it was a comfort to have been able to predict this and to know that my experience was in the normal range for accident victims.

Keep Others Informed

The example set by the paramedics is a good one. They inoculated me with a prediction about how I would feel later on. They knew I would feel worse, and they were experienced enough to disclose this to me so I wouldn't needlessly grow alarmed at the increasing level of pain.

They said: "You'll really start to feel this accident later tonight, but that's normal. You'll be OK."

People usually appreciate knowing what is yet to come, even when the events are less than happy ones. My dentist pointed out to me that he couldn't use anesthesia as he fitted my crown, because I needed to have enough sensitivity to tell him whether it provided a comfortable biting surface. At one point, he said, "This is as painful as it is going to get, Gary." I recall telling myself as I winced, "I can handle this." Dr. Shinto appreciates that patients have a strong desire to stay informed about what is happening and what is yet to come, especially when they're in the midst of a lengthy procedure.

Simply put, it is a great comfort to know what is going on. By keeping others informed in this way, we show the same respect toward them that we would want to be shown toward us.

Organizing the Content of Our Sensitive Communications Using PEP

We could be the most empathic-sounding people in the world, but if we don't seem to know what we're talking about, we'll sound foolish. The best way to dramatize our credibility is by sounding authoritative.

This doesn't mean that you should bellow out everything you say, as if you're making great pronouncements. Credible people are believable largely because they sound exceptionally well organized. Experts don't necessarily have more facts than others. What they do have is better command of their facts. They are able to express them better, because they are organized. So if you wish to sound like a credible expert, strive to sound organized.

I'm going to share with you a marvelous format for expressing your ideas in an organized way, especially if you're under the gun or communicating in a hostile or sensitive climate. It is called the PEP format, and it has three parts: point, evidence, point. The first thing PEP has us do is make a point. Usually, it is a declarative statement. The second step is to support the main point with three statements of evidence. The third step is to repeat the main point. We'll use a term such as *therefore* or *so* and tag it onto the original point.

I used something similar to the PEP format when I introduced the late-shipment example at the beginning of this chapter. You may recall that I said:

> *"Hello, Mary? This is Gary Goodman. I'm sorry, but I wanted you to know that our shipment is running a few hours late. I've been in touch with the driver and he has promised that it will definitely be there by four o'clock, OK? Again, I'm sorry for any inconvenience, and thank you for your business. Bye."*

PEP is embedded in the middle of this paragraph. My main point is "I'm sorry." Then, after explaining why I'm sorry, i.e., because of the late shipment, I repeat the statement that I'm sorry, before thanking the customer for her business.

This is a very casual or relaxed use of PEP and it's perfectly acceptable to use it this way. But there will be times when we'll want to sound much more crisp in structure. We could take the same example and embellish it a bit to make it sound more orderly.

> *"Hello, Mary? This is Gary Goodman. I'm calling to apologize for three reasons.*

> *"First, I'm sorry, but your shipment is running a few hours late.*

> *"Second, I'm personally disappointed in our performance because our on-time record is almost flawless, and I didn't want to let you down.*

> *"Third, I'm especially concerned because I understand this is the first time you have used Goodman Shipping and I don't want you to come away with the impression that this is the typical result you can expect in the future.*

> *"I've been in touch with the driver and he has promised that today's delivery will definitely be there by four o'clock, OK?*

> *"I want to apologize for any inconvenience, and thank you again for your business. Bye."*

What can we say about this more formal example? It certainly is longer, isn't it? In a sense, this is a virtue, because it makes our explanation sound substantially more weighty than the shorter version.

It also sounds like I really mean what I'm saying, and that I've thought it through before calling. This should send a clear message to the customer that she's important enough for me to take the trouble to consider how she'll react to a late shipment. I'm saying her opinion of Goodman Shipping's performance is vital, and that we take our mistakes seriously and we correct them.

Why Is PEP So Effective?

PEP works because it is a very *simple* format. Once we have selected a main point or theme, we know how we'll begin our little talk as well as how we'll end it. This should come as a great comfort to any speaker who is worried about how to begin or wrap up a tight and credible explanation.

Centuries of experience have proven the sequence of PEP works. In the Middle Ages, it was used by preachers to organize sermons. At that time, it was referred to as "The Little Method." In the military, it is the favored method for delivering briefings and training. Speakers are taught to: tell 'em where you're going; go there; and tell 'em where you've been.

When naturally expressive folks have the facts as well as the passion to articulate them, they intuitively reach for something like PEP, because it enables them to make a claim and then quickly support it.

PEP Is a Natural for Informing or Persuading

PEP can easily perform dually as a communication device. The same format can inform or persuade, depending upon the mission.

For example, let's say a dissatisfied customer has implied that she is prepared to take her business elsewhere. We could try to dissuade her in this manner:

"Ms. Haimoff, we hope to continue earning your business because of these benefits:

"First, we're going to place you in our VIP Club, which will enable you to take advantage of unadvertised specials.

"Second, we're going to give you an unconditional 15 percent off all of our products and services anytime.

"Third, we're going to provide you with the best service in town.

"So, we hope to continue earning your business, OK?"

This is overtly persuasive because we have disclosed our desire. It is nearly the equivalent of saying, "You should keep your business with us for these three reasons," which, by the way, would be a perfectly acceptable PEP point. It would fit nicely into the example I just gave you.

Sometimes, we want to inform a customer about how to do something. PEP can help here as well. Let's imagine that a customer has heard about the VIP Club and wants to know how to become a part of it.

"There are only three steps involved in joining our VIP Club.

"First, do business with us each month, for twelve months in a row.

"Second, spend at least $250 each month.

"Third, fill out a one-page application form.

"After you've completed these three simple steps, you'll belong to our VIP Club!"

Mr. Spock Would Love the PEP Format

"Star Trek" character Mr. Spock would say that PEP is a great format because it makes nearly anything we say seem "merely logical." Looking at the most recent example, I'm sure you'll agree.

What if the customer who inquired about the VIP Club thought that she had been unfairly excluded? How would you respond if she accused you or your company of being biased in its inclusion procedures? PEP could certainly help you to straighten her out because it clearly sets forth objective criteria for membership. It says if you do these three things, you'll be admitted, period.

PEP Says, "We're Not Making This Up as We Go Along!"

An aura of fairness or objectivity is very important to cultivate when dealing with customers or anyone in business. It not only diminishes conflicts but it also can help avoid them altogether. We never want to convey the impression that we're making up our policies and procedures as we go along. Everything we do should seem well thought-out and carefully considered.

By supplying three reasons or statements of evidence, PEP makes us sound thorough. As a format, it insists that we supply good reasons to support our assertions. Thus we don't just bark out proclamations in imperial ways. We explain why things are the way they are or should be as they should be.

Occasionally, We May Have to Improvise

I suggest you take the time to formulate some PEP capsule responses for the most challenging situations you face at work. By having them on hand, you can summon them as the need crops up. (In Chapter 6, I'll help you by applying PEP to the twenty-one most-difficult customer and client situations.)

But occasionally, even if you are quite prepared, you'll face circumstances where you'll need to improvise on the spot. Fortunately, PEP is also a fantastic tool for sounding brilliant under fire.

Let's look at its mechanics a little more carefully. I've already mentioned that if you know your main point, you're almost halfway home, because you're going to end your PEP talk with almost exactly the same point. So once you have your point, all you really need to be concerned about is generating your evidence.

Imagine that your boss has unfairly accused you of leaving the office early to attend to your own personal business. He said, "You always seem to be skipping out of here early, just when the work is piling up!" You would be shocked, of course, but what would your first impulse be, even if you have never heard of the PEP format? You would probably feel like blurting out, "That's not true!"

By having PEP at your command, you can say essentially the same thing but sound composed and authoritative:

"I'm sorry you have that impression, but I put in a lot of time.

"I'm here nearly every day until six o'clock or I stay substantially later.

"I make it a goal to finish whatever I'm working on before I leave.

"If I ever have to leave early, I obtain advance permission and I always make it up.

"So I put in a lot of time."

Don't Just Disagree—Argue the Opposing Viewpoint!

The previous PEP talk sounded very powerful, didn't it? It refuted the accusation, supported the refutation, and ended on a strong note by repeating the refutation. So it followed the PEP sequence perfectly.

But this reply was made even more powerful by the inclusion of a significant persuasive strategy. The accused didn't settle for proving the point that she or he wasn't skipping out when the work was piling up. The person turned the accusation on its head by trying to prove the diametrical opposite—that she or he is nearly always there.

Whenever you can do it, try to dispel misconceptions by proving their opposites. If someone argues that it's nighttime, you should respond that it's actually daytime. The more dramatic the accusations, the more completely you must shoot them down and "take no prisoners."

But why do you have to be so insistent? It's an unfortunate fact that if you're less than wholehearted in your defense, you'll implicitly concede that there's some truth in the argument that has been leveled against you.

You've heard of demagogues who sway the masses by repeating one big lie. Because it is only weakly refuted, if at all, it starts to stick, and people are swayed into believing it. So please don't fall into that trap, especially if you're wrongly accused of something.

Be instantaneous, be emphatic, and be thorough in your response. And by all means, use the PEP format!

You Don't Have to Shout

I should note, however, that even in this kind of career-threatening situation, you should try to keep your cool. Shouting won't help your cause. In fact, here's what you should be thinking, second by second, as you respond to a provocation.

First thought: I've just been wrongly accused of something. Refute it, but sound polite and composed. Say, "I'm sorry, but . . ." and then state the opposite of the accusation. Use a single phrase . . .

Second thought: That sounded good. Now support it with my first reason.

Third thought: Cool, that worked. What's my second reason?

Fourth thought: I'm rolling, now. What's my third reason?

Fifth thought: Beautiful! Just repeat my original point and I'm outta here!

Sixth thought: It worked! Yee-hah!

Does that seem to be a lot to think about when you're being held under the gun and you have to reply without hesitation? It does, but it's just a passing perception. Once you have practiced using PEP you'll be able to do what I do with seminar audiences. I ask them to throw topics at me, and without pausing, I make a main point, support it with three forms of evidence, and then smoothly return to my point. Some people think my ability to instantly respond is nothing short of genius, but PEP does the heavy lifting. All I do is work through the six-step process I've described.

Try it, and I'm sure you'll be sold on it as well.

What Is That "I'm Sorry, But . . ." Introduction?

Do you remember at the beginning of this chapter I noted it's important to handle the emotional agenda before proceeding to address the informational one? Well, that's what I did by starting the last PEP example with the phrase, "I'm sorry you have that impression, but . . ."

Technically, this is called a transition phrase, and it's very useful whenever we need to bridge from other people's statements to our responses. I'm sure you would agree that it would sound too blunt and combative to flatly attack the accuser by saying: "You're wrong! I put in a lot of time!"

By using "I'm sorry you have that impression," we sound dignified and polite. We also soften the blow, which could threaten someone's ego if we rode roughshod over his or her contention.

Transition phrases are crucial in another respect: they buy us time to think up and compose our PEP talks on the spot. Without a smooth transition, we are inclined to blurt out something unduly argumentative or irrelevant and ill-considered.

You should memorize these transition phrases:

- *"Well, I appreciate that, but . . ."*

- *"Well, I respect what you're saying, but . . ."*

- *"Well, I know what you mean, but . . ."*

- *"Well, I would be surprised if you were at this point, but . . ."*

- *"Well, I understand that, but . . ."*

Transition phrases are simple devices. They all tend to sound alike because they function in exactly the same way. Quite nicely, they give you permission to control the conversation and to say what needs to be said.

The initial *Well* alerts the other party to the fact that you're going to talk and so he or she should tune in to what is coming. It's also an informal word, which sounds friendly.

The middle part of the phrase is actually a temporary agreement with the listener. It says, "You may be right—to a point, . . ." but then you quickly about-face.

The word *but* is the beginning of your refutation. You follow it quickly with a PEP talk, which fully delivers your contrary viewpoint.

You may be concerned that by seeming to even temporarily agree with the listener, that person will get the wrong impression, or this tack will weaken your yet unstated viewpoint. It won't.

The temporary agreement in the transition phrase is intended to arouse a feeling of goodwill and openness in the listener. After all, if that person expects to hear nothing but a hostile contradiction from you, what will be his or her natural tendency? It will be to stop listening, right? So you earn goodwill and an opportunity to be heard by temporarily agreeing, or at least by seeming to agree. I see this as the equivalent of saying, "You're personally OK, but your statement is wrong." Or to put it differently, "You can stay, but the bull has to go!"

Summary

This chapter has provided the organizational skeleton over which you can construct the best responses on the spot to challenging business communication situations. You've seen how we need to address the emotional agenda of a listener before dealing with the informational agenda. You've learned the art of the apology, how to sound empathic, how to use the three-part PEP format, as well as how to use transition phrases.

The next chapter will show you how to level the playing field with your boss. You'll learn to negotiate raises, improve working hours, increase your employee benefits, and accomplish a number of other positive outcomes. In short, you'll find new ways to enjoy your work while deriving from it the best of all possible advantages.

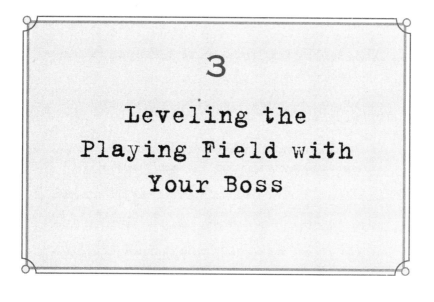

3
Leveling the Playing Field with Your Boss

Do you feel confident and optimistic when you consider asking for raises in pay?

Do you feel comfortable trying to speak the boss's language?

Do you have a firm grasp of the seven things that every boss wants from his or her employees?

Do you know the ten most common phrases you can use to start negotiating for more money?

Do you know the best vocal tones to use when negotiating with your boss?

Can you cite the key reasons your employer should support flex-time and job-sharing?

Can you clearly state why it would benefit your organization to offer better health plans and retirement programs?

Do you know how to diplomatically get reassigned to a new boss?

Do you know what to say to keep your boss from flirting with you?

Do you know how to quit or what to say during an exit interview?

Do you know how to ask for a positive reference letter?

Do you know how to get a positive reference, even if you've been fired?

IF YOU SAID no to any of these questions, never fear! By the time you've finished this chapter you'll have a good handle on all of these areas. Specifically, this chapter will show you how to effectively say these things to your boss: I want a raise; I'm overworked!; I can't do overtime; I want flex-time; I want job-sharing; I need more benefits; I want a new boss; don't flirt with me or harass me!; I've been head-hunted; I quit; and I need a reference.

Masters and Servants No Longer

What is it about communicating with our bosses that makes many of us feel insecure and helpless? Why do we dread the idea of asking for a raise in pay or for a meaningful change in how we perform our jobs?

Here's a clue: did you know that what we presently term "Labor Law" used to be called "The Law of Master and Servant"? That's right, managers and business owners were thought to be completely in charge of the three basic elements of an enterprise: land, capital, and labor. Before legislatures and courts set forth limitations, industrial "masters" used to be able to call nearly every shot that affected workers' lives—even away from the job site. Legally required minimum wages were unheard of back then, as were mandatory workplace safety precautions. Today, we shake our heads at such primitive conditions that were nearly universal a few generations ago. Yet the fear remains, if only below the surface of our consciousness, that employers might act arbitrarily and suddenly take away our security.

Never Fear! You Have Much More Power than You Think

You've probably seen a number of movies or read fairy tales about gentle giants who don't know their own strength. They are held captive or controlled by others because they are convinced of their weakness or helplessness. But once they discover their hidden resources, they never shrink back to their former dimensions.

I was riding on the San Diego Zoo's tour bus past the giraffes when the guide shared an interesting observation about these giants: "You'll notice there are no walls to keep these large creatures enclosed. If they wanted to, they could roam throughout the park," she said with a bemused tone. "Do you see that eighteen-inch trench that surrounds the exhibit area? They could easily walk over it with their long legs, couldn't they?" she challenged. "But they're so afraid of falling that they won't even attempt to cross it."

Let this illustration be an inspiration. The equivalent of a mere eighteen inches could be all that stands in the way of you leveling the playing field with your boss!

Speak Their Language

An essential secret to getting what you want from bosses and managers is to think and communicate as they do. Here are the seven things they want, as a general rule:

1. They want reasonably happy employees. They don't want to show up each day and have to face disgruntled workers who could "go postal" on them.

2. They want to look good and seem effective to *their* bosses.

3. They want to fulfill, and if possible, exceed their unit's objectives.

4. They want to earn profits for their companies.

5. They want to feel liked by their staff.

6. They don't want to appear as if they're wimpy or "soft touches" for any and every employee request.

7. They don't want to incessantly renegotiate the working arrangements they have with you. This means you can only go to the well and extract changes infrequently.

As long as you're willing to take their points of view into consideration before you make a request or a demand, you'll be more likely to win the concessions you want. But if you approach the process as if you're only concerned about yourself, you'll lose, sooner or later.

Now, let's get down to specific scenarios.

"Boss, I Need a Raise."

Let's critique the language that can be used to negotiate an increase in pay. Here are the ten most common phrases people use to ask for a raise.

1. *"I'd like a raise."*

This is a polite request. Its virtue is its succinctness. But there are a few problems with it, as you may have sensed. First, the operative verb is *like*, as in: "I would *like* to win the lottery." *Like* tends to cause the other person to think: "Yeah, wouldn't we all!"

The second problem with this request is that it doesn't contain a proper sense of *urgency*. I don't mean to imply that you should burst into your manager's office and blurt out: "I have to have a raise or I'll lose my apartment!" By urgency, I mean the type of need that is current, real, and needs to be addressed in the near term. As we proceed through the following examples, you'll see more clearly what I mean by urgency.

2. "I could really use a raise."

This is better, isn't it? The operative verb is *use*. Obviously, you would be saying that there is a practical purpose to which additional funds will be allocated. The verb *use* makes your request seem less frivolous than if you used *like*.

I also think some degree of urgency has been ushered in with the emphatic word *really*. You're pointing out that this is a real request and you expect some genuine consideration of it.

3. "I need a raise."

Better, still. How come? It's ultrabrief and to the point. It also sounds like a conclusion that you've reached after much deliberation. Also, it seems very urgent, partly because it uses the strong, hard-to-misunderstand verb *need*. There's no nonsense in this statement.

It does have a downside, however. Because it is so blunt, it can come across as an ultimatum, where the "or else" tag line is read into the statement by the boss. Typically, our superiors feel threatened by ultimatums because they seem to be power-grabs.

Your tone of voice will determine whether you appear to be acting reasonably and responsibly as you articulate your request, or if you appear to be brazen and a threat to the operation. For example, if your tones rise as you say, "I need a raise," ending on a peak, it could sound like an ultimatum. Here is how it would appear, tonally:

raise."

a

need

"I

To make the same statement sound less threatening, yet quite powerful, do it in a monotone, where your tones stay at the same level with each word:

"I   need   a   raise."

Please try reading these examples aloud to hear the effects. Ask yourself which one you would rather hear if you were hearing the request.

4. *"I'm going to have to get a raise."*

This is definitely an ultimatum, isn't it? The words that leap out at the listener are "have to." This statement is almost thoroughly urgent. In fact, the only way you could further amplify the urgency would be to add the words *this minute*, or *today*.

I'm not terribly fond of this phrase, because it seems to imply that you'll quit if you don't get immediate action. If you have another job lined up, that's one thing. But if you don't, avoid this approach.

5. *"I deserve a raise."*

This is another phrase to avoid, not because it misspeaks how you feel, nor because its content is untrue. You may feel you deserve a raise, and indeed, your work history might support this feeling. However, this phrase can make you sound like you're whining. Worse, it implies an "entitlement" frame of mind. *Deserve* carries an emotional connotation that suggests something rightfully yours is being wrongfully withheld. It reflects an adversarial, you-against-the-company mentality, which tends to scare managers.

6. *"I have earned a raise."*

If you are going the entitlement route, this statement is more acceptable because it focuses not upon something emotional, like deserving a raise, but upon provable performance. This phrase implies that you are going to offer evidence of good works to support your assertion, which is a positive way to handle a negotiation of this type.

7. *"Another company has offered me a position at a significant raise in pay."*

This is a very strong bargaining statement. It is certainly going to raise questions such as:

"What company is making the offer?"

"What are they offering you?"

"Did you contact them or did they contact you?"

"Are they offering you a different position?"

"What did you tell them in reply?"

"What do you want us to do?"

"Haven't you been happy here?"

Naturally, if your current firm doesn't value your work, they'll wish you the best of luck and many will call the security department to walk you to the door! In most cases, your statement, and the discussion that follows, will have the impact of an ultimatum. It will tell your boss to "fish or cut bait." You won't be allowed to resume your old duties at the same level of pay—at least not for long, because management will infer that you're unhappy. So they'll either ante up and raise your pay, or they'll lose you.

Let's assume for a moment that they do raise your pay, give you a fancier job title, or sweeten the pot in some way. Once you have discovered your "market value," and you've experienced the power of negotiating from strength, you and your bosses will inevitably wonder how long it will be before you come back to the bargaining table. Anticipating this, your company may let you go now to the higher bidder. This could be in the hope that they'll be able to replace you with someone who won't realize his or her market value and who won't make them jump through hoops to keep him or her happy.

8. *"I would like to discuss what I can do to earn a significant raise in pay in the near future."*

Bosses dislike ultimatums—we know this. But they also despise surprises, especially sudden personnel-related ones. This is what makes the What-can-I-do-to-earn-a-raise? approach so attractive. It seems to provide the manager with the luxury of a little time before having to fork over the bigger bucks. But if you examine the request carefully, there is still a fair amount of urgency being communicated. You are saying you want to see the increase in the "near future."

This approach has several strengths. It opens a discussion with the manager. This implies that both parties are going to participate in making the raise in pay a reality. It also places you in a favorable light because you are accepting responsibility for performing in a manner consistent with "earning" the increase. Finally, the framing of this statement removes from consideration the opposite thesis, that there's nothing you could do to improve your lot. If this were the case, the manager's verbal or nonverbal demeanor would disclose it, and you would be on notice that you should go improve your fortune elsewhere.

9. *"Are there additional responsibilities I can take on here, or a different job opportunity here that will enable me to qualify for a raise in pay?"*

The "What can I do?" operates in this overture, too. But unlike the last example, which was much more open-ended, here you are asking for new tasks, a new title, or a new job under the roof of your current employer. These are specifics that will motivate the listener to think about what you can qualify for.

Moreover, there is always the option of not giving you new tasks, but simply delivering a raise in pay, as a way of addressing the request. I also happen to like this request because it is fashioned as a question, and as such, it doesn't threaten. At the same time, once it has been uttered, the manager is on notice that money is on your mind and some action will need to be taken soon in order to keep you happy and on board.

10. *"What's the one area that you would have me improve in so I could justify earning a raise in pay?"*

Again, you have the strength of expressing a desire to do something in order to warrant getting something. But instead of asking for new responsibilities, this approach asks the manager to identify an area of weakness that needs to be shored up.

I like this because it accomplishes four things:

(a) It is a reality test of your performance, and you could consider the feedback to be a mini-evaluation. If there are perceived negatives in your work habits, you'll hear about them.

(b) Assuming you hear profound negatives, this will tell you not only that you can't expect a raise but also that your career is in potential jeopardy. This feedback might be a sign that it's a good time to update and circulate your résumé. Better to know this sooner than later.

(c) It is impressive to a manager when an employee requests criticism and feedback. This approach could be seen as a true sign of maturity.

(d) You may very well hear the one point of constructive criticism that you're asking for and this could make you much more valuable to your firm as well as on the open job market.

"Help! I'm Overworked!"

Instead of being willing to take on more duties for higher pay, you may find yourself in a position where you want fewer duties, especially if you find you're not meeting deadlines and performance targets. This is a particularly sensitive topic, because you don't want to seem uncommitted to the success of your firm or to your career. Additionally, you don't want to develop a reputation as a slacker, who shirks responsibilities and shifts responsibilities to others.

I consulted for one company that assigned special projects to its executives on a regular basis. According to my sources, it wasn't sufficient to do one's official job and move up the career ladder. You had to accept one special project, and sometimes two or three, to be considered a viable part of the management team.

This put executives under extraordinary pressures. Here's how clever ones cope.

- *They ask for help and for helpers.*

If your tasks are multiplying out of control, you need to step back and think through what is essential for *you* to do. Use what I call the Must-it-be-me test to evaluate the necessity of your involvement.

For example, let's say your company has decided to make personal contact with five hundred inactive accounts. You would ask yourself, "Must it be me who has to make all five hundred contacts, or can others do as good a job or better?" Framed this way, you can see that this task could be divvied up among ten or twenty people, each of whom could contact twenty-five to fifty accounts on the list.

- *They constantly ask themselves, "What is the highest and best use of my time and skills in this project?"*

In the inactive accounts project, the executive's highest and best use might be in scripting the conversational outline that associates could use to make as many contacts in as little time as necessary. Also, the executive could develop guidelines for the content of the messages to be left when callers reach voice mail instead of people.

In other words, planning, guidance, and coordination would be the highest and best uses of an executive's time in this special project.

• *They communicate effectively with their managers regarding assignments and their roles in executing them.*

It is up to you to communicate effectively with your superiors in order to get the resources you'll need to accomplish various tasks. Your proposal might sound like this:

> *"I've thought through the inactive accounts project and I've developed some numbers. If we have five hundred people to contact, we can assume that about 150 phone hours are required to accomplish this. Considering you want these clients to be contacted within a one-week time frame, this means thirty phone hours per day need to be dedicated to this project.*

> *"I can put my ten people on it, but because three hours per day will be taken up by this project, they won't get their regular duties done as well. So here's what I propose to do to bring the project in on time:*

> *"I'll borrow ten people from another department. I'll add them to my ten, and each will put in an hour and a half per day on this project.*

> *"We'll need to pay them overtime because we don't want to cut into their regular working day. This will take $20 per phone hour, or a budget of $3,000.*

> *"As an alternative, we can outsource the calling to a service bureau, which will charge us $35 per phone hour plus a setup fee. In that case, I would monitor their work.*

> *"Which option do you prefer?"*

Renegotiating Your Duties

You don't have to be some high-muck-a-muck to negotiate the best uses of your time. Wherever you are on the corporate ladder, you should involve your boss in prioritizing your duties. Let's say you're over-whelmed with responsibilities and you just know that some are going to fall through the cracks. How can you alert your manager to this state of affairs and renegotiate your duties? Try this:

"Bill, I want to discuss the projects I'm working on to make sure we get done what really needs to get done. As you know, I have three assignments: (1) The inactive accounts project, (2) the roll-out of the new mutual-fund training program, and (3) the development of the new advertising campaign. I feel like I'm moving in a hundred directions at once, so I want to hear which of the three is your top priority right now, and which one is the least critical to you."

"They're all important."

"I appreciate that, but which one is the first among equals, so to speak?"

"The new ad campaign, I suppose. Followed by the inactive accounts project."

"Very good. The reason I ask is that I know I can bring in the ad campaign, and quite possibly the inactive accounts project, but the training program may not get done by the end of the quarter, unless I can get some other people to help me out. Can the training program be set back to the second quarter?"

"I suppose, but I don't like this slippage on meeting our time targets."

"I agree. So would you like me to put someone else on the training program, or would you prefer I got to it in the second quarter?"

"Why don't you do it next quarter . . ."

"OK, I appreciate it."

"I Can't Do Overtime." If you're on a flat salary, you may be expected to perform uncompensated overtime as a part of your job. For example, lawyers in large firms realize that they typically have to bill about sixty to eighty hours per week to keep their jobs and to be in line for promotions.

There used to be a funny sign in an advertising firm in Venice, California: If You Don't Come in on Saturday, Don't Bother Coming in on Sunday! This made the all-too-real point that working long hours, possibly seven days a week, is part of the culture at that company. The sign was a jocular warning to clock watchers: "If you still think time belongs to you, then you have no future here."

You need to ask yourself if you have signed on with the right outfit. Are you at home with an organization that expects your number one, number two, and number three priorities to be the job? If so, then overtime is really an oxymoron. There's no such thing as overtime. Just not enough time, ever, to donate to the firm. On the other hand, if you're working at a typical company, which realizes that you may have a family life you would like to support, or that you actually have outside interests, then you can negotiate temporal expectations.

Of course, I should point out that today's companies really want to enjoy the best of all worlds. When their profits are tight, they want to operate with skeleton crews, and when profits grow and orders back up, they resist hiring new people, preferring to stretch their current staff to the max or even to pay overtime until the demand eases. You may be facing an unwritten rule that says, "If you want to stay aboard, or qualify for raises and promotions, you'll help us adjust to these feasts and famines and not complain."

So this makes a negotiation about overtime delicate, to say the least. I thinks it's best for all concerned to *fully articulate and make explicit the expectations.* When you feel that you're being expected to stay late, for extra pay or not, and that this is unofficially becoming a part of your job, you should step up and have a chat with your manager.

"Milt, things seem to have been getting busier around here."

"Yes, they have. We have a lot of work to do."

"I've noticed that I've had to stay late simply to keep up, and there's no end in sight. Are we planning to hire more people to handle the volume?"

"We would prefer not to, to keep our costs down."

"I appreciate that, but I'm going to need some help, because staying late is cutting into my personal time and my other commit-

ments. I'm willing to do what I can, every now and then, but I need to know if you're thinking of making my job permanently require ten hours."

"No, I wouldn't say that."

"Can I count on some help, or a letup in the volume?"

"Sure."

"I appreciate your help with this."

Note that the employee threw a bone to the boss by mentioning a willingness to help out "every now and then." This is a small concession to make in order to show that the employee is a team player, is flexible, and can be counted upon in the occasional pinch. At the same time, the employee communicates that the occasional pinch is very different than a long-term squeeze.

"But We're Willing to Pay You Overtime!" What if the boss is willing to pay overtime, or the equivalent, at least until normal operations resume? What then?

This makes it harder to turn down additional hours—no question about it. But let's look at the previous conversation to see if the same basic talk will work for the employee.

"Milt, things seem to have been getting busier around here."

"Yes, they have. We have a lot of work to do."

"I've noticed that I've had to stay late simply to keep up, and there's no end in sight. Are we planning to hire more people to handle the volume?"

"To keep our costs down we would prefer to pay you overtime, if we have to."

"I appreciate that, but I'm going to need some help, because staying late is cutting into my personal time and my other commitments. I'm willing to do what I can, every now and then, but I need to know if you're thinking of making my job permanently require ten hours."

"No, I wouldn't say that."

"Can I count on some help, or a letup in the volume?"

"Sure."

"I appreciate your help with this."

The strategy seems to work, whether the employee is offered over-time pay or not. That's a sign that the strategy should prove to be very useful.

"I Want Flex-Time." Over the course of our careers, our time prefer-ences can change quite dramatically. In our early twenties, we may be ready, willing, and able to put in seventy to eighty hours per week. When I simultaneously worked full-time and went to college full-time, I put in over one hundred hours weekly. It was stressful, but achievable.

But by the time I had a family, my desire to burn the candle at both ends flamed out quite quickly. I realized I would have to rearrange my priorities if I wanted to have a fulfilling family life. So I cut back on my travel time and trimmed my workload considerably.

You may realize that driving your child to school is one of life's greatest little pleasures. But you also realize that you can't be a happy chauffeur and arrive at your job by 9 A.M. Something has to give, so why not renegotiate the time you need to be at the work site?

"Bill, I would like to find a way to spend a little more time with my daughter, and I think I can do this by driving her to school in the mornings. If I can start here at 9:30 and work until 5:30, then I can pull it off. Are you open to that?"

Unless your job is to open the vault at a bank, or some other time-sensitive post, you should be able to work some flexibility into your schedule. I think if you show a compelling reason, and I believe time with family qualifies, then you should receive positive consideration, especially when you show your willingness to extend the day by the same amount of time.

"Boss, I Would Like Job-Sharing." Job-sharing is harder to pull off. When you job-share, you divide one position into two components, which two people perform fifty-fifty. Shirley might come in from 8 A.M. until noon, and Bill could pick up from 1 P.M. until 5 P.M.

On paper, job-sharing benefits both employer and employee. Employers get the benefit of two experienced people. They can assign tasks based upon each individual's strengths. Moreover, when one is out with the flu, the other may be able to fill in full-time.

Employees can enjoy professional careers, high occupational status, and interesting work, but not have to commit to a full-time arrangement. Parents of infants and young children report that job-sharing allows them the chance to see their kids and to keep their job skills current.

So how can you ask for job-sharing, and more important, get approval for it? I believe the best way is to sell the idea by taking full responsibility for its success. In other words, if you're willing to assure your manager that it will work or you'll return to full-time status, you have the best chance of making it happen.

Here's how to approach it:

"Bob, I wanted to do a little planning with you so there could be a smooth transition after I have my baby."

"Good idea."

"I would like to make solid commitments to my child and to my career, and I think we can figure out a way to do that. Have you heard of job-sharing?"

"You mean where two people do the job of one?"

"Right. It's a real benefit to employers and to employees. Employers get two well-trained people who bring different skills to the job. So it's like getting two sets of skills for the price of one. There's also a feeling of security knowing that one can fill in right away for the other in an emergency.

"Of course, it's a great tool for new parents, like me. I can make a contribution at work, keep my skills sharp, and not have to compromise having a strong bond with my child.

"Here's what I propose: With your permission, I'll see if there's someone in-house who wants to job-share with me. If so, we can both speak to that person and see if there's all-around compatibility. If no one is in-house, I can do a search outside, and we

*can interview. Assuming we find a good fit, I'll train the person
and get him or her up and running before I go on maternity leave.*

"Can we pursue this?"

"I Need Better Employee Benefits"

You may be one of many millions of workers who aren't covered by
health insurance or other benefits. We're going to see how you can
negotiate better benefits with a minimum of pain.

First, let's put the term *benefits* into perspective. A benefit sounds
like something extra, doesn't it? If a paycheck is the cake, then a benefit sounds like mere frosting—a bonus, a spiff, a perk, a goodie. It's
nice, but not essential.

Well, let's straighten that out, right now: benefits are money. They
are a cost to employers in the same way that wages, salaries, and rents
are all costs. And they are an advantaged form of income to you, the
employee. In fact, benefits are better than money, in many cases.

What do I mean? If an employer provides you with health or life
insurance, it may be a tax-advantaged proposition for you. You don't
have to earn gross dollars, then pay your income taxes, and then from
your remaining personal money, have to fork out for insurance. In other
words, it is a form of tax-free compensation for you. So, depending
upon your tax bracket, you could be getting a real break. Your accoun-
tant can tell you how much this adds up to each year, in dollars and
cents. Whatever it is, consider it "found money."

Therefore, it pays handsomely for you to derive as many benefits
as you can from your job. It also pays to improve upon the benefits
that you have. If you're already covered by a health plan, but dental
or optical coverages are excluded, you may want to lobby for a new or
modified plan that includes these items.

I suggest you do your homework before you approach management
with the idea of making sweeping changes. Contact a number of health
care and insurance providers on your own to see what they offer for
companies of your size, and compare their rates.

Then set an appointment with your boss.

*"I've been interested in improving my health care coverage so that
it would include dental and optical. When I looked into rates*

for individuals they were really expensive, so I did a little checking on group rates for companies our size. I've found that we may be able to add these coverages for slightly more money than we're paying Lunar Life. Possibly, we won't even have to pay anything extra.

"I would like permission to develop this further and to ask for specific bids. I know everyone on the staff would appreciate it, and it can't hurt. Is this OK with you?"

Let's say you don't have any coverage. I would broach the topic of adding benefits this way:

"I've been shopping for health care coverage, but the quoted rates for individuals have been really expensive. Is there a way that I could get my insurance through the company instead?"

Benefits Benefit Employers as Well. Although there are some socially conscious companies that do their best to offer a host of benefits, most firms don't do this out of the goodness of their corporate hearts. They do so because it makes sense, as in dollars and cents.

By offering benefits, companies have much greater chances of retaining quality personnel. I did a survey of companies involved in customer service and inside sales, and I found a staggering connection between offering health plans, 401K retirement plans, and other pluses, and keeping good people aboard. The companies that had rampant turnover had done nearly everything they could to *not* offer benefits, and they paid a very high price in terms of lost human capital.

Dreamy Benefits from Dreamworks. Dreamworks, the studio founded by Steven Spielberg and associates, offers its employees a number of benefits that go well beyond the ordinary. At their Glendale, California, "campus," employees are treated to free lunches in the cafeteria as well as to a number of kiosks that dispense espresso, cappuccino, as well as more exotic coffees.

Why do they go to such bother and expense? Employees voluntarily work longer hours because they're so comfortable. Additionally, they collaborate more freely across departments because there are so many easily accessible indoor and outdoor conference areas.

By delivering these nifty benefits, Dreamworks is establishing a culture that is attractive to creative people, who are always in high demand in Hollywood. In tight labor markets, more companies should look into creative benefits to accomplish the same goal.

"I Want a New Boss!"

Asking for reassignment to a different department can be a very touchy subject, especially if your motivation results from not getting along with your current supervisor. How can you break this news without being punished for it, or worse, being fired for doing so?

This is a chance to use *metacommunication*, which we will discuss in Chapter 6. As you'll see, it is a process where you discuss the problem openly, hoping this will clear the air for both parties. Let's see what metacommunicating could do for you in this sticky situation.

"I would like to do everything I can to be effective in my job, but I get the feeling that we're miscommunicating in some way, which I would like to correct, if possible. Are there certain areas where you feel we're not on the same page, so to speak?"

"Well, I'm not sure if we're connecting on some things, either, but they are hard to identify on the spot, if you know what I mean."

"For example, I got the impression that you weren't completely happy with how the inactive accounts project went, though you didn't say anything about it."

"Well, you and your team got it done, on time and on budget, but it seemed to me that you were kind of halfhearted about the project."

"I don't know how you got that impression. I was stressed with a number of tasks at the time, including my regular duties, so I asked for some outside help. Is that what you mean?"

"Well, that's part of it, but I don't know . . ."

"I would like to see what we can do to work more effectively together, but perhaps it might be better if I were reassigned to a

different department or we found a new opportunity for me. Should we look into that?"

"I suppose we could."

"I hope I would receive your support and a positive recommendation from you if we go that route."

"Sure, of course."

"Well then, I'll mention this to human resources so when something comes up we can take a look at it, OK?"

"Yeah, that's fine."

"Thanks. Good talking with you."

We could beat around the bush or try to drum up some excuse for wanting a new job, but I prefer the direct, metacommunicative approach. In this example, the employee tried to start a dialogue about the communication gaps that might be troubling the relationship, but the supervisor didn't seem genuinely interested in exploring this area. It was as if she or he was saying, "This isn't going to improve. I just don't get along with you."

In such a case, it makes sense to try to align with another department and a new manager. Even if you had to leave the company, this could serve you better than working for an unappreciative manager who isn't going to mentor or promote your career.

"Don't Flirt with Me or Harass Me!"

Sexual harassment is illegal under federal law.

It may involve making unwanted sexual requests as an implied or express condition of getting or keeping a job, receiving raises or promotions, or performing one's work. It can also include promoting or allowing a hostile atmosphere where gender-related jokes, verbal assaults, innuendos, or other uncomfortable conditions are present.

Many companies have explicit policies to deal with offenders and to discourage this conduct; however, it still exists. If your manager, or even your peer or a vendor, makes unwanted advances, you should put him or her on notice that they are not welcomed. If they persist, you should bring the matter to the attention of human resources. If your firm is small, you should contact an attorney conversant with labor and employment law, or contact the closest office of your state's Employment Development Department or the U.S. government's Equal Employment Opportunities Commission.

What can you say to discourage this conduct but not seem unduly threatening? First, I suggest you ask the following question with an ultraserious tone:

"Are you flirting with me?"

This could be enough to get the individual to back off. If the person does retreat by saying, "No!" you can reply, "OK, good." That should be more than enough to tell the person that his or her overtures are unwanted.

But what if the person tries to probe into your personal life and intimate preferences? What can you say then?

"You're asking about personal matters that I keep private. They have nothing to do with my job, and I'm going to decline to discuss them, OK?"

If the person's misbehavior is chronic and unrelenting, you may have to spell it out:

"This talk about sex constitutes harassment. It's keeping me from doing my job, which is what I'm here to do. I expect it to stop right now. Understood? Thank you."

Again, if you're in an abusive environment, do yourself a favor: get help. Start inside the firm, and if it doesn't abate, go outside.

"I've Been Head-Hunted."

There is only one reason to tell your employer that a placement agency representative, a.k.a. a headhunter, has contacted you about an open position at another company: it is to bargain for a better deal where you are.

But as you can imagine, this is a delicate situation. Your current employer will resent the fact that someone has been seeking your services, probably on his or her company's time. She or he will also feel threatened that the work team is being stalked by competitors and by other poachers. Even if managers would be happy to see you leave, they would still be jolted by the experience that one of "theirs" has been contacted.

Your current boss is probably no fool. She or he realizes that it takes two to tango, and that any overture made to you wouldn't have sounded sweet if you were completely satisfied with your current deal. So they realize that you may be making a move—if not now, then in the near future.

Don't announce the fact that there's a fox in the chicken coop until you have secured a tangible *offer* from the suitor. Once you have that, let the bargaining begin!

> "Mary, I want to get your advice. I've received an offer to go to work at another company, and I want to get your input in evaluating it. I've been happy here, as you may know, but this offer deserves to be looked at."

> "What company is it? What are they offering?"

> "Well, it's another high-tech firm and not a direct competitor. They've offered me about 30 percent more than I make in cash, some improved retirement features, and a management title with a small staff reporting to me. What do you think?"

The Art of Quitting

Do you remember the old Neil Sedaka tune that oldies stations adore: "Breaking Up Is Hard to Do"? Well, breaking up in business can be just as difficult and emotional as parting company with a loved one, if we don't handle it correctly. So we need to take special care to manage our emotions and to make the experience as smooth as possible.

If we've been with a firm for a considerable amount of time, it's likely that we've developed positive relationships with at least some of the people we have worked with. We need to acknowledge this to them and to ourselves as a first step to communicating our intention to leave.

> *"Mary, I've enjoyed working here with you and with a number of people. That makes it difficult to tell you that I'm going to be resigning, effective in two weeks."*

"You're kidding? What are you going to do?"

> *"Actually, I'm going to take off for a few weeks or a month and get my bearings before I go into something else. I think I'm going to look for something in publishing, which is my first love. We'll see, but be assured that this isn't a reflection upon you or anyone else, and certainly not upon the company. It's just a matter of it being time to transition into something else. So if I can help you to train anyone else during the next few weeks, please let me know, OK?"*

"Sure, sorry to lose you."

> *"Thanks."*

What if you absolutely despise your boss and the company, and you think your associates should take a hike? Please don't say it. This is not the time to ventilate, though that may be exactly what your company will beg you to do if they schedule an exit interview with you.

The exit interview is really a fishing expedition, though it is positioned as a method through which the company can improve its operations and "prevent good people like you from leaving us in the future." Don't take the bait and think of this scene as one in which you should let it all hang out. You really, really shouldn't. Don't rat on your boss, or inform the human resources manager that your peers make far too many personal calls on company time and on the company dime.

Rather, tell them you've enjoyed this experience, you've learned, you've contributed, and you hope you've made a big difference. You're leaving behind a legacy of hard work and solid accomplishments. Remember, how you handle yourself during the exit interview will create the company's last and final impression of you, so make it a glowing one.

"But that's not true—if it were such a great place, I would be staying!"—is that what you're thinking? Please remove that thought from your mind, because it's not always true. Winners do well at a company and then move on to bigger and better things, if they can. It's normal. People don't depart only because they're unhappy.

Asking for a Reference

This leads us nicely into the matter of asking for a positive reference. If you want to have positive momentum in your career, a good reference is essential.

First of all, please notice that we are *asking* for a reference, and not simply expecting to receive one as the normal course of events. Asking is necessary, because it primes your backers for the very important role that they're going to play in helping you to secure your next position.

By explicitly asking them, you are also committing them to doing the right thing for you. Without this nudge, they could get lazy, or their impressions of you could change dramatically. How come? Have you ever noticed what happens when someone resigns from a job? After he or she is gone, the detractors come out of the woodwork and start a campaign of delayed character assassination. They may make statements such as these:

> *"You should have seen her sloppy notes in the computer—I've had to spend days just to make sense out of them!"*

> *"When I told his customers that I was taking over, they nearly said, 'Hallelujah!' You could hear how relieved they were."*

> *"I don't know about you, but to me it seems so much more calm here now that Shirley is gone. Isn't that funny?"*

Get Them to Praise You (in Writing, if Possible!)

As you're telling your boss how wonderful she or he has been, and how cool the company has been to work for, try to get your boss to praise you in turn.

> *"I hope you've found me a capable and productive associate, and someone who has been pleasant to work with."*

"Definitely, you've been great. Hate to lose you."

"That's nice to hear, and I know future employers are going to want to know that as well. Could I ask you for a favor—could you just give me a paragraph that says I've been capable, productive, and pleasant to work with, and that you hate to lose me? That would be great, and it would save you time because people wouldn't have to get you on the phone just to say the same thing."

"I suppose so, sure."

"Great, could I pick that up at the end of the day, or would it speed things up if I type it up for you?"

"OK, why don't you do that. It'll save time."

"Sure, I'll stop back around four, OK?"

"Yeah, fine."

What If You've Been Fired?

The last example presumed you were a model employee your boss really didn't want to lose. What if you've been fired or laid off? Will this stuff still work?

Why, not? In fact, you'll have a greater need for a positive reference in that case, yet you'll probably be concerned about asking for one. Don't be. Here's how I would handle that situation:

"I realize that the company chose to let me go, and I'm not going to argue about that. In fact, I wish the company well, and you, too; I hope you feel the same way about me."

"Of course, we do."

"You could make it a lot easier for me to find my next job if we could agree upon the contributions that I made when I was aboard here. Would it be fair to say I was pleasant to work with? And did I perform reasonably well? And was I always neat and punctual, and took my duties seriously? Would you feel comfortable

sharing these strengths with anyone who might contact you about employing me? I would really appreciate that."

What if the boss says she or he isn't comfortable saying nice things about you? I would simply respond with this:

"If you aren't comfortable saying positive things I would appreciate it if you would simply supply any callers with the essentials of my employment: how long I worked here, my salary, and so forth. In other words, can I count on you to not say anything that would keep me from getting my next job?"

In other words, be practical. Try to elicit their praise in writing. If you can't get it in writing, settle for verbal praise. If you can't get praise, accept an agreement to not prejudice your future job prospects. As one of my uncles once said, with respect to negotiating: if you can't get five, you must take two!

Summary

This chapter has shown you how to communicate effectively with your boss. You've seen how to negotiate raises, a modified workload, less overtime, flex-time, job-sharing, more benefits, a new boss, a flirtation- and harassment-free environment, head-hunting situations, resignations, and the generation of positive and helpful job references.

In the next chapter you'll learn to dramatically improve the relationships you have with your peers at work. You'll be given tips for handling some of the most annoying people, including the loudmouth, the gossip, the vicious competitor, the slacker, the maverick, the rat, and the informal leader.

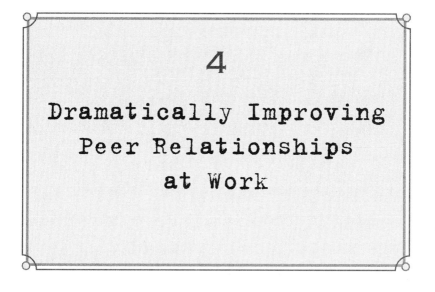

4

Dramatically Improving Peer Relationships at Work

Would you like to know what your communication rights are in the workplace?

Have you ever wanted to muzzle an office loudmouth?

Have you ever wished you had a device for halting a runaway blabber?

Would it feel good to restrict a conversational rambler to one topic at a time?

Have you ever longed for a tool that could defang the most vicious office gossips?

Do you wish you knew how to defuse a vicious competitor?

Have you ever resented the fact that a coworker doesn't carry his or her share of the load, and wanted a way to rectify the situation?

Do you wish you could trade an office maverick to another team?

Would you like a way to get your group's maverick to go along with the program?

Would you like to trap an office rat to keep him or her from telling on everyone else?

Would you like to get on and stay on the good side of your group's informal leader?

THIS CHAPTER WILL show you how to deal with the behavior of annoying peers. These include blabbers, ramblers, and loudmouths; office gossips; vicious competitors; slackers; mavericks; rats; and informal leaders.

*   *   *   *   *   *   *

Helen can't get through an hour without jabbering about "those bozos in accounting" or a myriad of other associates. Jerry does most of his work in slow motion, and Thelma marches to a drummer only she can hear. Like an eight-year-old, Milt delights in reporting every one of your transgressions to senior management. And Shirley won't rest until she has torpedoed all of your initiatives, so she can ease into your job when you stumble.

How can you get any work done with these motley folks at your side and frequently at your throat? Actually, it's easier than you may think, providing you use some of the techniques that we'll discuss in this chapter. Before dealing with these wrongdoers, let's discuss some of your rights.

Your Rights in the Workplace

Wouldn't it be nice if we could mentally and emotionally turn off the unpleasant behaviors of our peers at work? Unfortunately, this isn't possible or practical with some of the worst offenders. Therefore, we're stuck in the potentially irksome position of having to change their behaviors.

There are several steps in making effective changes. The first step is to appreciate that you have certain *rights* in the workplace, irrespective of your formal occupational title. Here is a short list of them:

• *You have the right to enjoy an atmosphere that is free of incessant distractions.*

Distractions are interruptions in your thought processes or in the physical execution of your duties that are caused by your fellow workers. For example, if every afternoon you have to hear nonstop partying in the cubicles next to yours, you're being incessantly distracted.

This means you can't do the job you signed on and are paid to be doing. Your coworkers are preventing you from fulfilling your employment agreement. Moreover, if you can't perform at peak levels, you'll miss out on raises and promotions that you could otherwise earn. No one, and I mean no one, has the right to take food off of your table or deny you or your family career benefits.

Please note that I have used the phrase "incessant distractions." This is important, because all of us will occasionally be distracted, and we have to live with that. Incessant distractions are relatively nonstop—they recur, and they dominate the psychological atmosphere as well as a huge communication space.

• *You have the right to expect cooperation from your coworkers.*

An organization is more than a collection of individuals who are looking out for themselves. It is a team, like it or not, and players have to enable their teammates to play their positions. By sharing work space and resources, you're entitled to expect a certain baseline of behaviors from your peers.

• *You have the right to expect professionalism from your coworkers.*

Professionalism means a sense of duty to perform one's job at the highest possible level. People who willingly adopt this attitude subordinate their private lives to their organizational roles, at least while they're at work. They may be Little League coaches, amateur singers, or coin collectors during their personal time, but when they're at work, they're at work. Certainly, there can be occasional small talk about outside interests, but it is relegated to the back burner. When we're at work, we're acting for our companies, and our roles are to perform our jobs. Everything else should be incidental.

 • *You have the right to expect a fair reward commensurate with your contributions.*
   What happens when we have to go to work each day and sit across from someone who does half the work we do, yet receives exactly the same paycheck? We feel an emotion that is known as *contempt*. A sense of outrage over unfairness, our contempt occurs when we see that an "inferior" is getting as much, or even more, than we're getting. Slackers stimulate this emotion that can be incredibly corrosive. After all, we think, "Why should I bust my butt while they sit on theirs?"
   Thus we grow discouraged, and everyone loses, including the company. To avoid this fate, you should be prepared to articulate what your rights are, to yourself, to your supervisors, and to offenders. By being convinced of your clearly defined rights, you'll carry yourself with special authority and dignity as you assert them.

Asserting Your Rights

The second step toward improving the working atmosphere is in preparing your remarks. How can you come across in a reasonably pleasant way while getting your point across? Let's try a few potential scripts to see how they'll work.

Loudmouths, Blabbers, and Ramblers

Meet Marv. He's the one who speaks in an abnormally loud voice, on the phone and off. He shouts out his hellos, good-byes, and intervening comments. How can we give him a communication adjustment?
   Take him aside, and try this:

"Marv, you know, you have a great voice! Have you ever done any radio?"

"Actually, I thought of it once . . ."

"Well, you could. Your voice is big and clear. The reason I've noticed is that it has seized my attention whenever you answer the phone. It's such a loud voice that it kind of rattles me and I forget where I was in my task. Would it be too much of an intrusion if I asked you to tone it down a bit? I like it, but it's distracting me, if you know what I mean."

"Yeah, no problem,"

"Thanks."

Do you want to see people light up? Compliment their voices. I've never seen this fail to warm up the coldest fish.

In the preceding case, a structural formula called the "sandwich" was used to impart the request to Marv. The sandwich follows this three-part structure: start with a compliment, slip in the critique, and then end by repeating the compliment.

Of course, some other things were done that are worth noting. The speaker clearly told the offender about the loud behavior and its impact, noted that it "seizes" her attention, and "rattles" her. And then the speaker asked for a specific result by suggesting Marv "tone it down."

It would be hard for Marv to miss the point being made. There is also something implied that is essential to get Marv to own up to changing. The speaker suggested that Marv is in control of his voice because it is nearly radio-announcer caliber. Hey, he's the next best to a professional, so he can do it—right?

Marv's loud, but at least he gets to the point when he speaks to customers and to coworkers. What can be done about Florence, who never seems to get to the point? Is there a way a coworker can straighten out this potentially hopeless rambler?

With ramblers, you have to be even more intrusive, simply to focus them. So I suggest you use transition phrases followed by focusing questions. Here is a sampler:

"Well, I know what you mean, but what are you trying to tell me about the Henson file?"

"Well, that sounds interesting, but what's the bottom line with respect to the Applegate situation?"

"Well, that's great, but when it comes to what we're going to do from here, can you net it out for me?"

Another approach is to apologize for interrupting, and then to ask the focusing question.

"Sorry to interrupt, but how much are we willing to pay out to put this situation behind us?"

In each case, the speaker maintains politeness. This is important so you don't needlessly ruffle feathers—your associates' or your own.

Blabbers are folks who give you far more information than you asked for, or than you need. In a way, they show off and try to impress us with their depths of understanding and command of various topics.

So I suggest you briefly play to their egos, which are crying for gratification:

"Izzy, you seem to know a lot about this, but the only thing I need to know is whether Quark makes a good graphics program for the Macintosh."

"Bill, in light of your experience with home audio systems, what's your opinion of Bose—in twenty-five words or less?"

The Gossip

Gossips spread rumors about people. Stirring the pot of human emotions, they delight in seeing to whom they can serve up the worst cases of heartburn. Why do they do these dastardly deeds? They're bored, and they need some excitement. They also feel important by sharing secret "news" and by distracting the victims of their phony headlines.

Generally, the subject matter of rumors pertains to our private lives. As I've said elsewhere in this book, private matters should remain private. Moreover, we have a right to enjoy a good reputation, free from innuendo or even outright defamation.

Gossip can definitely damage our careers. For example, Trudy is an attorney for the civil service. She is always neatly, if not stylishly groomed. She never complains about money or having to pay the bills on a public sector salary. Betty started a rumor that Trudy didn't need any money because her husband was rich. In fact, according to Betty, Trudy was so well-off that she didn't really need to work at all, and she would probably "fly the coop" at any time.

Whenever better jobs opened up, Trudy's applications were never taken seriously because she was perceived to be little more than a temp, despite the fact that she was a capable and dedicated attorney. After making some inquiries, she discovered the damaging rumors and tracked them back to Betty, whom she confronted.

We shouldn't ignore gossip. If it persists, people will come to believe that there must be some validity to it, as in the expression "Where there's smoke, there's fire." So we should combat it quickly and vigorously.

"Betty, it has come to my attention that you think I'm rich and that I don't need to work. Where did you ever get that idea?"

"I didn't say that!"

"Whether you did or not, I'm going to straighten out this rumor, OK? First of all, I'm a professional and I'm 100 percent committed to doing a good job, and I do a good job, day in and day out. No one here works harder than I do. To suggest that I don't have to work, or that I might quit at any time isn't true and it's damaging my reputation.

"Second, my personal life and my finances are private; they have no bearing upon my job performance. Is that understood?"

"Sure—OK."

"If I hear any more rumors, I'm coming straight to you with them. If you hear any more, I would appreciate it if you would straighten them out before they reach me, OK? Thanks."

In this scenario, Trudy is straightforward and succinct in confronting Betty. Trudy doesn't say right off the bat that Betty has been spreading rumors. Instead, she says, "It's come to my attention that you think I'm rich and that I don't need to work." By characterizing the problem this way, Trudy is saying that Betty's opinion is the problem—

not that she has decided to spread it around as a rumor. This is a constructive way of confronting someone because it focuses upon the initial problem—the perception. Straighten that out, and there's no need to get caught up in calling someone a gossip, which can make him or her fly off the handle and become unnecessarily defensive.

Of course, Trudy went beyond this by saying that she was going to confront Betty with any more rumors that she hears about herself. This says, "I know you're behind these rumors." But then she tags on a line that allows Betty to save face: "If you hear any more, I would appreciate it if you would straighten them out before they reach me, OK?" This "deputizes" Betty to join the posse in tracking down and stopping offensive rumors in the future. Throughout this talk, Trudy comes across as absolutely serious and determined to put an end to the destructive gossip. That's the way you should sound, if you find yourself in this situation.

A closing question: did Trudy ever explicitly say that she wasn't rich? She doesn't have to do so to have the moral authority to stop rumors. The content of a rumor could be technically true, but it is inappropriate since the rumor could be used to wreak havoc upon the subject's career.

The Vicious Competitor

A good number of psychologists and sociologists believe that people, as well as other species, are inherently competitive. There will always be pecking orders, they say, and to really appreciate our creaturehood, we should get comfortable with the idea that at work, at home, and at play, we almost always seem to be keeping score.

Of course, unbridled competitiveness, especially in the workplace, can become destructive. Instead of perceiving our actual competitors to be other companies that vie for market share, we see our coworkers as the adversaries. We can become obsessed with showing them up and with trying to prevent them from reaching their goals.

Let's say there are two managers who have people reporting to them. If they're involved in destructive competition, they might say these sorts of things to each other:

"I'll bet you $100 my team will beat yours this quarter."

"You guys are never going to match our sales, so why don't you just throw in the towel and end the suspense?"

"Has Cindy finally figured out how to do order entry? I have to say, you got the short straw when we recruited the last batch of employees."

"Maybe we should trade teams for a quarter or two. You can see what it feels like to be with a winner, while I can sharpen my turnaround skills."

Each of these statements intends to demoralize the competitor. And if we hear them often enough, they'll probably work. That's why we have to make these competitors stop.

The best way to handle the vicious competitor is to tell him or her, quite explicitly, that you're not going to play the game. At the same time, you'll want to remind this person that competing with each other isn't what you're in business to achieve.

You both have *real* competitors in the *real* world with whom you need to square off. How can you have the energy and focus to fight them when you've beaten each other up? As Sun Tsu, the ancient sage says in *The Art of War*: "Victory with exhaustion means defeat in the battle to come."

Think about it. Wouldn't your real competitors fall all over themselves with laughter if they heard you were fighting among yourselves? In fact, wouldn't they pay industrial "spies" to create such dissension and havoc in your company?

You all have much more worthwhile things to do. Tell your associate:

"Bill, I'm not competing with you or with your team. Our competition is Sharp, Ricoh, and Canon, so let's gear our efforts to defeating them, and not each other, OK?"

The Slacker

Slackers are people who don't do their fair share of the work. This means we need to do some of their work for them, or at least deal with the uncomfortable feeling that they're earning pay for work that they aren't doing. Slackers also preclude our departments from qualifying for team bonuses because such poor workers depress our production averages. So they are potentially taking money out of our pockets.

Whose responsibility is it to confront slackers and to make them conform to performance targets? Officially, it is the supervisor's or manager's, but he or she can't always be counted upon to put the rubber to the road.

I consulted for a company that harbored a notorious slacker. Doug only did about 15 percent of his official duties. During the remainder of the working day he served as a missionary for an obscure religious cult. He would actually phone customers and try to convert them to his beliefs!

Managers were aware of his antics, but the legal department warned them that they could face a lawsuit if they fired him. So they tried to isolate him, by moving his desk to the outer edge of his department so he couldn't "infect" his coworkers.

His coworkers didn't see this move as an optimal solution. What would you have done?

One thing you can do is apply the very powerful tool of peer pressure. While Doug may feel that management can't touch him, he could react completely differently to the idea that he is letting his associates down.

So you can confront him this way:

"Doug, how's it going?"

"OK, why do you ask?"

"Well, it seems to me that you aren't very happy here."

"How did you get that idea?"

"Well, I suppose people who like their jobs do everything they can to complete them, each and every day. But you only seem to get a small portion of your work done, and yet you're a capable person. So I figure it has to be attitude, am I right?"

"Well, I try to keep my attitudes to myself."

"So do I, and that's normally fine. But if you don't do your work, and you're logged off the phones for most of the day, we have to

take the calls that would ordinarily go to you. In other words, we're doing your job for you, and that's not fair, is it?"

"Well, uh, I don't know what to say . . ."

"That's OK. You don't have to say anything. Just do your job, and we'll forget all about this, fair enough?"

"Yeah, OK."

"Thanks, I appreciate it."

I should point out that Doug's behavior was so persistent and so egregious that he deserved termination. He had received incremental discipline and ample chances to change his conduct. But let's return to the legal department's concern about not wanting to be sued.

My client's company is public, and as such, all filings of lawsuits against it must be reported to the Securities and Exchange Commission. So even a frivolous suit may appear to be a threat to profits, and once reported to the investment community, it could depress the value of stock shares.

A legal department's number one priority is to reduce risks; it is not to produce profits or a motivated working team. So it wouldn't be sensitive to the fact that Doug's blatant lack of productivity demoralized the rest of the team, as well as made management seem ineffectual and timid to many of its other employees. The legal team figured that keeping Doug on board was cheaper than letting him go.

I disagree with this assessment. The costs of defending a suit, in financial terms as well as in disruption and distraction, can be great. But it's important for managers to draw the line when it comes to appropriate versus inappropriate conduct, and prevailing in a suit can make this point and discourage spurious litigation in the future.

The Maverick

Mavericks actually are organizational misfits. They relish doing things their own way and get great glee out of breaking the rules. They tend to make awful employees, because they would rather show up a system's flaws than create a better, more flawless system. In baseball, the maverick would be the player who comes up in the bottom of the ninth in a tied game, with one out. The coach flashes a signal to do a squeeze bunt, which is calculated to tie the game. The maverick pretends to miss the signal and swings away, hitting a long single that scores two runs and wins the game.

Every maverick I've ever known in business subscribes to this principle: it is better to ask for forgiveness than for permission. Mavericks make great entrepreneurs, because they can scan the landscape for opportunities and then pounce upon them. But they are really uncomfortable doing routine work, where uniformity of methods is highly valued.

So let's say you have a maverick on your team, but instead of making the clutch hit in the ninth after you have called for a bunt, that person is more likely to strike out. What can you say?

"Margi, I know you like to do things your own way, and sometimes you come up with very creative solutions. But most of the time, these tactics miss their marks entirely and simply waste your time as well as ours.

"We need to be marching in the same direction or working off the same page, if you know what I mean. It's like we're in the brass section but you keep looking for a violin to play. So I'm going to ask you to play by the rules and do things the way the rest of us do them. If you have suggestions, make them during our team meetings, and if they look good, we'll all adopt them, OK?"

What if Margi doesn't take this hint to heart? Then it may be time to play hardball:

"Margi, we've spoken about how you like doing things your own way, and how this can be counterproductive. Because you decided to print the last proposal with our own in-house tools, instead of farming the job out to Kinko's, we wasted at least two days. The sales manager got really teed off, and he asked me what was going on here.

"You are a creative person, but there may not be enough creative outlets in this position for you. Have you ever considered going out on your own or joining a more creative company?"

"No, I haven't, really."

"Well, you definitely should, because you shouldn't be wasting your talents around here, and we can't keep allowing you to do your own thing. Understand?"

"Yeah, I guess so."

"Let me know what you decide to do, and let me know if I can be of any help, OK?"

I hope these texts sound comfortable to you, because they should. They are honest, direct, but still upbeat. Instead of simply announcing the problem and ending on that note, the speaker suggests a solution, which is for Margi to look for a creative position elsewhere, and the speaker even offers to help.

I believe that most organizational misfits are clueless as to why they are wasting time being square pegs at a job made of round holes. I also believe that most misfits are highly energetic people, who genuinely want to make contributions, but are stuck in jobs that are, well, boring.

According to recent surveys, 75 percent of attorneys would not choose to go into law, if they could choose again. Many dentists can't wait to retire so they can pursue, get this, sculpting! There are many folks across the occupations and professions who would be happier doing something else, somewhere else. So if we make them aware of this fact, as it pertains to them, we could be performing a great service.

The Rat

The rat is a person who reports each and every one of your shortcomings to management. If you blow it in any way, the rat will notice it. Like most toadies, this creature believes that she or he gains favor by being the eyes and ears of management.

What the rat doesn't realize is that ratting on you won't actually elevate his or her career. In fact, by wasting time as spies, rats fail to pursue more important matters, such as taking on more responsibility for their own development. Moreover, they make poor managers, because instead of creating an open communication atmosphere, they do the opposite. They make people recoil into postures of self-defense.

I would handle rats in the same general way that we dealt with gossips—confront them:

"Judy, I was called on the carpet this morning for ordering too many pizzas for Jill's birthday party last week. The only person who was aware of this little mistake was you, and it seems you felt compelled to report this to Jim, right?"

"I didn't report it, but it did come up in conversation."

"It came up? How?"

"I don't remember, but anyway, you did order too many pizzas, didn't you?"

"That's not the point, Judy. We all make mistakes and I'll be glad to own up to mine. But you seem to take it upon yourself to report everything, large or small, to management, and this means you create a distrustful atmosphere. In other words, that's against creating a team spirit."

"I disagree. I simply call them as I see them."

"Judy, who appointed you the company rat? Do you actually think you're going to advance here by ratting on your coworkers? Managers may listen to you, but they know they can't trust a rat. Be a real human being. If you see some piddling error, look the other way, and we'll all get along a lot better. Otherwise, we're going to have to play the same game, and your flaws will start being reported. Every one of them, every time—in Technicolor. I hope we've come to an understanding. Have we?"

"Uh, uh, I don't know what to say . . ."

"Good, let's get a fresh start by going back to work and doing the jobs we're really getting paid to do."

This is fairly confrontational, but what can I say? I believe that the more secretive the rat tries to be, the more up-front and emphatic we need to be. What's at risk if we take this approach?

Well, Judy could report *this* conversation to management. But what could she say? That the speaker threatened to report her failings if she persisted in reporting others'? Turnabout is fair play, right? Could she complain that the speaker called her a rat? Sure, but this is just as likely to raise smiles as eyebrows. All in all, I think this conversation will most likely get her to pause before she offends again.

The Informal Leader

The last of the problem colleagues we're going to discuss are the informal leaders. These are the people in any working group who set the communication tone and the pace of the work.

They're the ones who will come down on slackers for underperforming and for making the work group look bad to management. They'll also tell associates when they're overperforming and therefore subjecting the group to raising its output.

No one elects informal leaders. They don't get any extra pay or formal recognition. In fact, they wouldn't admit to having any clout if managers accused them of it. They like it that way, because they can wield authority without having to accept formal responsibility.

But informal leaders matter so much in any working group that savvy managers will run their new initiatives by the informal leaders first to get their endorsements, before rolling out changes to the group at large. So, because of their power and pipeline to management, you really want to get on and stay on the good side of informal leaders. They can make your working days very pleasant or hellish.

The best way to work with them is to know who they are. Here's how to spot them. Generally, they are individuals who have been working in the group the longest time; people to whom others give eye contact whenever there's a question of policy or procedure that pops up; and the first ones to ask you about your background and interests after you have come aboard. Take their questions as an opportunity to get them to give you the lay of the land:

> *"Ed, you seem to be very experienced here. What's the scoop when it comes to the output that's expected of us? And what should I look for and look out for?"*

If you've made an error, and Ed isn't the informal leader, he will probably say something like:

"I'm not really the one to talk to about that. Ask Mary—she's plugged into everything here."

"I will, thanks."

Of course, you would use the same overture with Mary that you used with Ed. It works, because it flatters and asks the magic questions: "How do I fit in here? Where are the land mines? Who and what should I look out for?"

By dignifying the informal leader's power and knowledge, you'll probably get the answers you need, and you'll become an instant part of the team. You'll be taken under the informal leader's wing. Until, that is, you screw up or threaten that person.

How can that happen? Well, you could have an ego clash by wanting to be the top dog yourself. There can't be two, so suppress that impulse. Or you might have a magnetic personality more compelling than the informal leader's, making the flock congregate around you and causing the informal leader to become jealous.

The way to stay out of the informal leader's way is by being a friend. Compliment that person. Build him or her up. Thank that person for her or his help. Tell that person you couldn't be as effective without him or her. In other words, if you're a natural leader, show it by being a good follower.

Of course, the ecology of the situation could change dramatically if you're promoted and that person suddenly has to report to you. We'll address this challenge in the next chapter.

Summary

This chapter showed you how to deal with the behavior of annoying peers. These included the loudmouth, the gossip, the vicious competitor, the slacker, the maverick, the rat, and the informal leader.

In the next chapter you'll receive a promotion. You'll be the boss who needs to communicate sensitively with your subordinates.

5

Communicating with Those Who Report to You, and Improving Relations with Those Who Don't

Do you feel uncomfortable giving formal criticism to those who report to you?

Would you like to learn a logical and comfortable format for conducting a feedback session?

Would you like a way to quickly and cheerfully take the chill off of a feedback session?

Would you like a technique, similar to PEP, that can help you quickly get to the heart of the matter?

Would you like to be able to clearly but calmly implement incremental discipline and issue performance-improvement warnings?

Would you like to be able to create clarity in defining and redefining performance objectives?

Could you use a method for discussing demotions so they have a good chance of being acceptable to employees and the company?

Would you like to have a succinct way of conducting a termination interview?

Would it help you to be able to elicit more productivity from employees without having to pay higher compensation?

Would you like a win-win method for getting the cooperation of other managers to help you to realize your objectives?

THIS CHAPTER WILL help you to do all of these things. You'll increase your comfort level in all employee feedback situations; use a logical format for organizing your discussions; sound cheerful, but businesslike; get right to the heart of the matter, no matter how sensitive; clearly and convincingly issue performance warnings; create clarity in defining and redefining employee performance objectives; provide workable demotions; succinctly conduct terminations; get more employee productivity, without paying more; and get the willing cooperation of your fellow managers.

*   *   *   *   *   *   *

When I was a young manager with Time-Life Books, I was paid the ultimate compliment by one of our top salespeople, who said: "Gary, I know I could earn more money somewhere else, but you make this an exciting and fun place to work. That's why I'm sticking around." Having fun and achieving at high levels should go hand-in-hand. After all, producing results is very enjoyable because we're baking a bigger pie for everybody. It's also fun to show ourselves how good we can be, and frankly, there are few things more enjoyable than seeing tangible proof of our value.

So as we begin our discussion of communicating effectively with employees, we should keep these basic thoughts in mind. Most of us work to put food on the table. But work is also an exercise in self-discovery. A manager's task is to help people to see, develop, and refine their strengths, while working around their weaknesses.

How to Conduct a Critique Session with an Employee

People need accurate and up-to-date feedback about their performances on the job. Professional managers schedule formal sessions with the people who report to them so employees can see how far they've come toward meeting or exceeding their objectives. These sessions also serve the purpose of maintaining open channels of communication between managers and their subordinates, but this is a secondary benefit of these encounters.

Critique sessions should follow an agenda consisting of three discussion points:

1. What objective did we set forth to achieve?

2. How well are we doing in achieving it?

3. Where do we need to go from here to achieve it or to achieve related objectives?

The best way to begin a session is by signposting this structure for the associate, after having broken the ice with a little small talk:

"Hello, Harriet! Please have a seat. How's it going? That's good. I've been looking forward to this meeting with you because you've had some time to dedicate to the inactive accounts project, and I want to catch up with you on that.

"Specifically, we're going to cover three topics: First, we'll revisit our objective for the inactive accounts project; second, we'll hear from you about your progress with it; and then we'll see where we can go from here to make the program even more solid. OK? Well, great . . ."

This is a cheerful but highly organized overture, and it should put the associate at ease. The manager says that he has been looking forward to the session. This sends a signal that he expects good things to come out of it. By signposting the three discussion steps, he also sends a comforting signal that he is not going to go on a fishing expedition for inappropriate information.

The next step is to review the performance objective:

"Harriet, as you know, we decided to contact our three thousand inactive accounts because we assumed two things. They have purchased from us before, and so it is easier and cheaper to reactivate them than to find completely new customers.

"We also agreed upon these targets: first we expected to have reached 90 percent, or 2,700 of these accounts by today; and second we also anticipated that we would reactivate at least 20 percent, or 600 accounts. So how have we done so far?"

The ball is now in the associate's court. She knows exactly what is being asked of her and precisely what kind of answer the manager needs to hear to do his job, and the session is only five minutes old. So he is in good shape. Let's hear Harriet's answer:

"Well, Gary, we're off target on both issues. We've only reached about 30 percent of the inactive account base. And of those 900 accounts, we've only reactivated 45 of them, or about 5 percent, so far . . ."

"So we're way off our projections. What went wrong?"

"We knew from the beginning that the database was old—in relative terms. Because we have a nationwide account base, we found that a lot of the area codes and phone numbers have changed since we last contacted the accounts, and they had to be updated. A number of companies merged or went out of business, as well. So my people have had to clean the list before they could even call into it, and that took a lot of time."

"I'll say! It's going to set us back several months. When did you first learn about these database problems?"

"We knew almost right away, and we started cleaning it just as fast."

"Did you think of bringing it to my attention?"

"Not really, I figured we could handle it."

"Well, I appreciate your self-confidence, but you made two errors:

"First of all, whenever you run into a major obstacle in meeting your objectives, you need to communicate that to me immediately. Second, you should generate a menu of alternatives that you can choose from to overcome the obstacle.

"In this case, we could have had a commercial 'look-up' firm clean and update our list with their software programs. It would have taken one week to do, max, without any significant distraction of our people.

"But let's turn to the second target, the one dealing with how many inactives we are reactivating. Why so few?"

"We've found that a good number of those we've contacted are already doing business with other companies. Some simply don't use our type of products anymore. A few have heartburn over a service issue or an accounting problem that they may have had with us, so they're not coming back."

"What are your people saying to get customers to come back to us?"

"Saying . . . ?"

"Yes. Are they offering any special discounts or talking up how we're carrying more products than ever before?"

"Not exactly. They're saying hello, finding out if there have been any unresolved problems with us, and sometimes they ask the inactives if they are buying from our competitors."

"OK, let's see if I'm tracking all of this. We still have 70 percent of the inactive accounts database to call. We also need to sharpen our sales skills so we can revive a much higher percentage of those we call. Are these the basic challenges?"

"Yes, I would say so."

"What additional resources will you need to complete this project in a minimal time with a better result?"

"I may need a different batch of people to make the calls!"

"Why do you say that?"

"My current team members just aren't salespeople. They're customer-service folks who are much more at ease handling inbound calls, answering customer questions, and the like. So I don't know if they would even do that much better if we handed them scripts to follow."

"Well, we can't recruit an entirely new team. How much time will it take to simply call through the rest of the database, putting aside any issues of increasing revival rates?"

"I would project that we would need another four months—possibly more."

"That's not going to cut it. Can we outsource this to a service bureau that will make the calls for us?"

"I suppose we could, but they're not going to know anything about our business or our customers."

"Given that your folks don't like to make these calls, I don't imagine outside professionals are going to do any worse. I would like you to develop a list of possible outsource companies we can use.

"Start with ten local firms. Have them send us their literature—overnight it, in fact. Do an initial screening of the ten and boil the list down to three. Then set meetings with them for Tuesday, Wednesday, and Thursday of next week. We'll try to award the business to one of them as early as Friday, OK?"

"Uh, sure—OK. I didn't think I was going to lose the program so quickly."

"This is how it works around here, Harriet. You're given the ball and it's OK to drop it occasionally—but if you do, you have to get your teammates to pick it up really fast so we don't lose the game.

"I do believe there's a lesson in this for you. Involve me in what you're doing, especially if you're hitting obstacles. Actually, you hit three of them: you ran late on the database cleaning, your reactivations were way below target, and your people were resisting the program. The third one is a killer. We can't afford to have people rebelling against the tasks they're being assigned.

"I would like you to identify some seminars or training institutes that you could attend in the areas of project management and managing change. Show me their literature, and we'll send you to the appropriate ones so you can get a better handle on managing special projects in the future, OK?"

"*OK.*"

"Let me know what you dig up on those outsources, OK?

"*OK.*"

"Good. Talk to you later. Bye."

Let's do a reality check. Did this session cover the three points that a critique session should cover? I believe it did. Participants reviewed the objectives and targets for the inactive accounts project, they discussed the project's results to date, and they covered what they need to do to bring the program to a successful conclusion.

If you follow this format in your performance appraisal sessions, you can't really go wrong. Of course, I should make one observation. What if Harriet had reported that she had completed the program as planned, on time and on target?

In that case, the third discussion point would have turned into words of praise for a job well-done, and a new objective would have been established, so Harriet would know what to work on next. In their subsequent meeting, the manager would then cover the same three-step process.

Implementing Incremental Discipline

It isn't much fun to reprimand or punish one's employees, but upon occasion, these negative reinforcements must be dispensed. And it doesn't do anyone any good to delay the day of reckoning or to sug-arcoat the bitter pills that must be prescribed.

In the dialogue involving Harriet, her manager did reprimand her for not consulting with him about the obstacles she was encountering in the inactive accounts project. His reprimand wasn't the overarch-ing purpose of their meeting, but a by-product of it.

What if Harriet emerges from the meeting with a hostile attitude about losing control of the program, and instead of immediately inves-tigating outsources, as requested by the boss, she stalls? Additionally, let's assume that she sets no appointments for Tuesday, Wednesday, and Thursday, and her boss only discovers this failure on Tuesday morning.

This kind of nonfeasance can put Harriet's job into jeopardy. But the boss can't get away with flatly firing her, even if he wants to do so. He needs to document the fact that he has issued proper warnings and that he has given her a chance to redeem herself.

A disciplinary meeting is an important component in the process of either getting the employee back on track or paving the way to a defensible separation. Here is what a special disciplinary discussion would sound like:

> *"Thank you for coming over, Harriet. I'm going to come to the point right away. As you know, I wasn't entirely pleased with the han-dling of the inactive accounts project, and I explained why in our meeting a week ago. I said you failed to communicate with me promptly when you met obstacles. Had we touched base, we could have overcome the obstacles with a few corrections. But as it is, we've lost a lot of time and we're not close to finishing the program.*

> *"In our meeting, I asked you to identify three outsourcing compa-nies that we could interview starting tomorrow. Only this morn-ing did I discover that we don't have a single interview set up, so it appears we've lost yet another full week. What happened?"*

> "Well, I couldn't find any outsources that seemed appropriate for this project."

> *"I know for a fact that there are at least a dozen well-sized firms in this city that make calls for hire—why, they've even contacted me over the years. You're saying you couldn't find any?"*

"No, I'm sorry."

"When did you discover you were coming up empty-handed?"

"Well, almost right away."

"And you didn't ask anyone else for help?"

"I suppose . . ., no."

"Harriet, there's a pattern in your conduct that needs to change immediately. First, you need to complete the tasks you're given, on time and on target. Second, you have to become a team player and less of an island unto yourself. Keep others in the communication loop, especially at the first sighting of trouble. Is that clear?

"I need to see immediate improvement, or we're going to have to arrange for a separation from the company. Consider this a formal warning. Also consider it a clear chance to change your conduct.

"Now, we need to get this inactive accounts project outsourced. Can you set up interviews for next week, or should I put someone else on it?"

"I'll do it. I'll do it."

"Fine, I want to get a report from you tomorrow afternoon, say at three o'clock, telling me of your progress, OK?"

"OK, see you at three."

"Very good. Have a good day. Bye."

Creating clarity is important in any meeting, but it's imperative in a meeting for dispensing discipline. Associates need to learn how they've erred, how the error has impacted others and the company; and that immediate improvement is required or further discipline will occur.

There's also a management adage that applies to the next step in the process: if you're going to *expect*, you have a duty to *inspect*. In the last scenario with Harriet, the manager decided to make an inspection within twenty-four hours, to ensure that the outsourcing project was well underway. This puts Harriet on a short leash, and it sends a signal saying management is absolutely serious about the necessity to get the job done.

Giving a Demotion

Let's say Harriet muddled through the outsourcing program, but she needed a lot of hand-holding. In effect, she demonstrated that she didn't have the maturity or the commitment to spearhead projects as is required of an effective manager. Moreover, every chance she got, she avoided signing up for the training programs that her boss had recommended.

Because she was an effective customer-service representative before receiving her promotion, she might be offered her old job back. This isn't an ideal move to make, but it might be a lot better from her point of view than being terminated altogether.

Let's see how such a demotion could be explained.

"Harriet, hello. Please, sit down. How have things been going for you?"

"OK, I suppose."

"Harriet, I want to see what we could do to improve the situation here from your point of view, as well as from management's. As you know, we have experienced a lot of slippage on some vital projects. First, there was the inactive accounts project, and then the outsourcing project. Finally, with a lot of outside help, we were able to finish things—but we were way off target.

"At this time, we feel reluctant to assign any more projects to you to lead. We feel you would perform better in a nonmanagerial capacity, as you did before you took over your present position. So we would like you to consider returning to customer service as a rep, until something else opens up for which you would be qualified. How would you feel about doing that?"

"My gosh, I don't know. I never expected this."

"Well, we appreciate that this is somewhat unusual, but we want to provide you with a chance to stay aboard in some capacity."

"It wouldn't be easy working as a peer with people I've been supervising. Plus, if you promote one of them and I have to be his or her subordinate, that would be very uncomfortable."

"I understand how you feel. I suggest you think about this overnight, and first thing tomorrow morning, come in and tell me what you've decided, OK?"

"OK. Bye."

This dialogue reveals some of the problems with demotions:

- A tremendous status loss occurs to demoted people. For many people, you either move up in a firm or you move out. Moving down is unthinkable.
- The next appointee who has to deal with a fallen manager has a problem: does he or she treat the demoted person the same as everyone else?
- Will the demoted person become bitter and secretly torpedo the initiatives of the new appointee, thus becoming an invincible informal leader?
- Will a demoted employee be able to adjust to what could be a major decrease in pay, as he or she assumes a lesser position?
- Will the demoted employee become a marked person—a perceived failure by others in the company—thus diminishing his or her ability to ever rise in the ranks again?

These negatives would seem to suggest that demotions should never occur, but there *are* rare situations in which they work well (see Case in Point on page 104).

The Termination Interview

Harriet has considered her boss's recommendation that she return to the customer service team as a rep. But she feels insulted and that she is being set up as a laughingstock. How could they ask her to even consider answering to people she has been supervising for over a year? It is preposterous!

But she needs the money, and she isn't going to quit. She decides to simply say no to the boss and see where the chips will fall. Here's how she approaches the matter and how the boss responds:

CASE IN POINT

SALES MANAGER BARRY

Barry rose through the ranks with a publishing company while he was attending college. Having started as a salesperson, he became the top performer in short order. When a managerial job opened, he was selected for it.

But as a leader he never reached the prominence he had as an independent salesperson. His boss asked him to consider going back to sales, which turned out to be a great move. Not only was Barry happier again, but he actually made more money than he made as a boss. His ego survived the adjustment, because, he said, "I never really thought of myself as a nine-to-five type."

"Good morning, Harriet! Please have a seat. So what have you decided to do?"

"I don't think it would be a good idea for me to be a customer service rep again. I say that from everyone's point of view."

"Well, where does that leave you?"

"I don't know. Perhaps there's another position that can be created for me?"

"No, Harriet, there isn't. I have nothing else I can offer you at this time. It's either the customer service rep position, or we'll have to arrange separation from the company."

"But that's not fair!"

"I'm sorry you feel that way, but we've done everything in our power to be eminently fair. You've been aware of your performance, and you've been given many opportunities to redeem yourself. Actually, we're under no obligation to offer you your old job back, but we're bending over backward to be as fair as any company could be.

"But now, we've reached the end of the road, I'm sorry to say. So please go immediately to human resources. I'll call over, and they'll help you to get your things and arrange for you to receive your pay and any other benefits that may be coming to you."

"I still think this is unfair."

"I'm sorry you feel that way. Good-bye, and good luck."

This may have seemed abrupt to you, but I would rather characterize it as being succinct. Don't waste a lot of time beating around the bush. Instead, when it becomes clear that you two have reached the end of the trail, you should say so and arrange to make the separation then and there.

Getting More Productivity from Employees Without Paying More

How can you get employees to willingly take on additional job responsibilities, without giving them immediate raises in pay? This challenge is constantly being faced by managers whose companies are trying to increase profits.

In a perfect world, we would be paid exactly for what we contribute to our customers and to our companies, and not a penny more or less. But no organization can deliver this kind of precise equity. Instead, there will be times when employees will deserve much more than their current level of pay, and at other times, they'll deserve much less.

As a rule, profitability requires that companies pay out less than they take in. After every expense is paid, including salaries and employee benefits, what's left over is considered profit. Healthy companies are those that have a lot left over. The firms that get into trouble are typically those that have difficulty maintaining their profit margins.

So it's natural for managers to want to get increasing amounts of output from their people. Sooner or later, some of the profits from added productivity will trickle down to the employees who are responsible for creating them.

These facts need to be explained to employees who are being asked to do more without being paid more. Here's how to do it:

"Ivan, nice to see you! How are you holding up, with all of the changes that we're going through?"

"OK, I suppose. It seems like a lot of people are getting the ax!"

"Well, you're still with us, fortunately. You've always done a very effective job, and it has made my job easier to do.

"As you noticed, we're reducing head count, but the workloads aren't going to be reduced. If anything, we're all being counted on to expand our areas of responsibility. How would you feel about adding the title of Customer Service Manager to your current one?"

"You mean, you want me to take Harriet's place?"

"Exactly. That group could benefit from your leadership, and we're only talking about adding ten people to the twenty you already manage."

"Why me?"

"It's logical, for one thing. You're the collections manager, so you're used to supervising phone work. Plus, your unit is right next door, so we wouldn't have to move you around. What do you think?"

"Is there an increase in pay?"

"Not right away, not in the cost-cutting mode that we're in. But down the road when things stabilize, I'm sure that would be looked upon more favorably. Right now, we need to tighten our belts, and managers are getting a chance to show that they can add to the bottom line by accepting more challenges and taking them in stride. In the long term, your enthusiastic agreement to

do this won't go unnoticed by senior management, and it will be a big investment in your career. Can I count on you to step up for us?"

"Sure, I guess so."

"Great. I'll set up a meeting with the customer service representative group for four this afternoon, and we'll make the announcement. See you then."

In the preceding example, the boss didn't have to get into the facts of economics with regard to profitability. But he could have, if the employee had balked about taking on the new duties.

Getting Fellow Managers to Support Your Initiatives

Let's take a look at how to get support from people who *don't* report to us—our fellow managers. Frankly, this process doesn't differ much from handling a good meeting with a subordinate. There are three steps to getting support:

1. The first thing to do is to announce your performance objective.

2. Next, specify what support you'll need from your counterpart.

3. Finally, set a target date for completion, and calendar a follow-up meeting.

    Here's how to do it:

    "Melody, I'm glad we could get together. Since I was appointed customer service manager, you can imagine how busy I've been, right?"

    "Me too."

    "This reorganization is making us all scramble, isn't it? The reason I wanted to get together is to see if we can pool some of our scarce resources to improve our respective teams. Your people in Technical Support spend most of their day on the phones, right?"

"That, and doing research, yes."

"I want to get some advanced phone skills training for my people in Collections and in Service. If we involve your twenty people in the training, we should be able to realize some economies of scale in negotiating with the vendor. This'll make the training more likely to be approved. Are you interested?"

"Sure, if it's solid training."

"Well, I'll set up meetings with three potential vendors, and we'll pick the most compatible one, OK?"

"OK."

"Let's target the first meeting for next Monday afternoon, followed by Wednesday and Friday afternoons, OK?"

"Sounds good."

"Good, I'll run it by the VP, and if there aren't any glitches, I'll confirm the Monday meeting with you."

Summary

This chapter has discussed the best method for conducting a positive critique session with a subordinate. You've also seen how to implement incremental discipline prior to terminating an employee, how to give a demotion, how to conduct a termination interview, how to ask a subordinate to produce more without immediate compensation, and how to get fellow managers to support your mission and department.

In the next chapter, we'll focus upon communicating with customers and clients. You'll be provided with techniques for handling the twenty-one most challenging customer service and client communication situations.

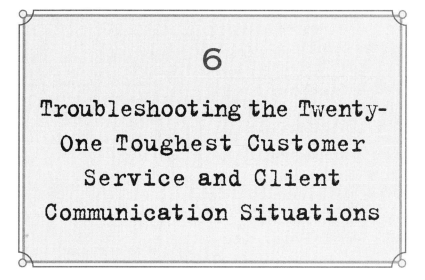

6

Troubleshooting the Twenty-One Toughest Customer Service and Client Communication Situations

How would you like to be able to gently but effectively break such bad news as:

> *"Your shipment will be late."*
>
> *"We're out of stock."*
>
> *"We've had a price increase."*
>
> *"You must pay a restocking fee."*
>
> *"I can't help you right now!"*
>
> *"You're in breach of contract."*

"You're lying!"

"We're substituting automation for human help."

"Don't yell or use four-letter words with me!"

"You're fired, Mr. Customer!"

"Your payment is late."

"You can't get credit with us."

"We blew it, but we want your business, anyway."

"You can't speak to my supervisor."

"You'll have to speak to my supervisor."

"I can't give you a refund."

"Let's not do lunch."

"Stop flirting with me!"

"Dear customer—you're demoted."

"We're canceling an event you wanted to attend."

"Our company has been sold."

IF YOU HAVE ever felt like running and hiding rather than having to deliver such bad-news messages as those listed above, don't worry! You're about to become a masterful messenger of such sensitive communications. In this chapter, you'll learn: to explain and to justify late shipments, out-of-stock situations, price increases, restocking fees, and your unavailability to help; to handle customers who breach their contracts or who lie; to explain the substitution of automation for human help; to discourage customers from using profanity when speaking to you; to "fire" customers with finesse; to collect late payments; to gracefully deny additional credit; to accept blame but still retain someone's business; to keep a customer from speaking to your supervisor or to steer the person to your supervisor, as the situation may require; to deny refunds; to avoid socializing with clients; to discourage flirting; to "demote" customers; to cancel events with a minimum of hassles; and to diplomatically announce the sale of your company.

Is There a Difference Between a Customer and a Client?

A number of people would say that there are vital differences between customers and clients. They would argue that to qualify as a customer, a person must:

- engage in a single transaction with them;
- which probably has a low dollar value; and,
- therefore, the value of a customer, relative to their overall revenues, is small.

By the same token, they would say that clients:

- engage in numerous transactions;
- which have a high dollar value; and
- therefore, the value of an individual client, relative to their overall revenues, is fairly large.

These distinctions could be useful in some contexts, but they're meaningless in terms of this book. I believe customers, even if they're short-term and their business generates relatively little profit, should be treated with the same degree of professionalism as clients are treated.

Perhaps this example will make the point clear.

On the way home from work you remember that you have a prescription to fill at the pharmacy, so you stop at a local drugstore. You walk to the rear of the store, you tender your doctor's note, and you're asked to wait while the prescription is filled. You're treated nicely. The pharmacist considers you to be a client, or perhaps a patient.

As you're leaving, you ask a store clerk where you can find breath mints, and the person leads you directly to the correct aisle.

Both experiences were smooth and enjoyable for you.

Did you hold the pharmacist and the clerk to different standards of politeness and helpfulness? Probably not. If you're like me, you wish to be treated well, irrespective of the labels "customer" and "client."

So, in the following pages, I'm going to use the terms *customer* and *client* interchangeably. The techniques you're about to learn are suitable to clients as well as customers.

"Your Shipment Will Be Late."

As they say, the best-laid plans sometimes fail, and we can find ourselves stuck trying to explain a policy or somehow justify a mishap. What are some of the best ways to do it?

Some would like to indulge a first impulse and simply announce the bad news:

> *"Hey, Bill—it's Gary Goodman. I just got word your shipment's going to be late, so hang in there. Talk to you soon, OK? Bye."*

If we shoot from the hip, we'll probably miss and hit ourselves in the foot. So we should be ultracareful in crafting our responses. The example notification is a problem for several reasons. First it's abrupt. There's nothing smooth in this little talk to keep a customer's feathers from ruffling. Second, the talk doesn't explain *why* the shipment is late. Was there bad weather in the East that held it up? Did the truck break down or the train derail? People appreciate hearing reasons that will explain the delay. If we don't provide the reason, our customers will infer that we simply messed up and forgot to get it out on time. They'll conclude that we are inept, and that won't make them feel warm and fuzzy about entrusting their cargo to us in the future.

Nor does this response forecast *when* the shipment will finally reach its intended destination. Wouldn't you want to know when you should expect the arrival of a delivery, so you could plan accordingly?

Finally, this talk contains no apology or expression of empathy for the inconvenience caused by the delay, and it doesn't provide an assurance that, if preventable, this sort of delay won't recur.

A more thorough and satisfying talk would sound like this:

> *"Hello, Bill? It's Gary Goodman. How are you? Good. I'm calling to let you know that unfortunately your shipment is running a little late because of that snowstorm on the East Coast. The blizzard closed some airports which is wreaking havoc on lots of our customers. We're expecting normal operations to resume later today, so that means you can look forward to delivery as early as tomorrow afternoon, say, between one and three. If there's any change, one way or the other, I'll update you ASAP, OK? Thanks for your patience, and thanks for doing business with us, Bill. Bye."*

Why is it better? Let's examine it.

Is it smooth? Does it seem to take the customer's feelings into account? I believe it does, because the speaker mentions right away that "unfortunately" the shipment will be late. He acknowledges the disappointment. The speaker leaves the conversation by thanking the customer for his patience and for his business, and telling him that he's important and the company respects him.

Did the talk explain why the shipment is late? It certainly did, by mentioning the snowstorm and the delayed flights.

Did it forecast when the delivery would arrive? Absolutely—between one and three the following afternoon.

Did the speaker have enough empathy to assuage any worries of further delays? Certainly—he said he would call if there was a change in status, "one way or the other."

Did the talk mention avoiding this problem in the future? It didn't have to, because the problem was due to bad weather.

By being so thorough, the speaker sounds like he is on top of the situation, and makes the customer feel that he chose wisely in doing business with this company. Moreover, this talk sounds very personalized, doesn't it? It sounds like the speaker is personally concerned for that particular customer's shipment. This idea is communicated by the use of the customer's name at the beginning as well as at the conclusion of the conversation.

Whatever You Do, Please Avoid These Pet Peeve Phrases

We should avoid using certain phrases and statements that are guaranteed to raise the hackles of most clients. Here are some pet peeve phrases that belong in the communication Hall of Shame:

1. *"You'll just have to wait."*

You can appreciate how tempting it would be to say this to a customer in the late-shipment case. But it's obvious that he'll have to wait, so why say it?

Moreover, people hate to be told what they have to do. It reminds them of angry parents who scolded them and proclaimed: "You'll have to clean up your room before you can play!" "Have to" is what linguists call a *mand*. You already know this word from its uses in other words, such as *command* and *demand*. Avoid using mands altogether.

2. *"You must put any complaints you have in writing."*

Another mand, right? Notice how forceful these phrases sound? It's akin to pushing people around with words. And what happens when we push people? That's right—most of them push right back.

By the way, many people are self-conscious about their writing. They suffer from the equivalent of stage fright when they are required to spell out their ideas. So if we can provide them an alternative channel through which to let off steam, they'll appreciate it.

3. *"It's not our fault."*

Who cares whose fault it is? The key is what we're going to do to solve the problem. In the shipping illustration, the speaker couldn't solve the weather nor open the airports, but he could still responsibly address the problem. He did so by explaining the situation, predicting when delivery would occur, and promising to stay on top of the situation and to notify the customer of new developments. That's far from avoiding responsibility with a not-our-fault cop-out.

4. *"That's not my responsibility."*

This is an attempt to personally weasel our way out of helping someone, while implicitly passing the buck to an unnamed associate. But it simply makes us sound gutless and unduly bureaucratic. When customers experience problems, they don't see an organizational chart of our company in their minds. They feel *anyone* who answers the phone or who will speak to them can assist in solving their problem.

5. *"You can't talk to me like this!"*

This statement is usually made by someone who has taken offense over something a customer said or the tone of voice a customer used. Unfortunately, this mand doesn't effectively alter a customer's verbal behavior, even if the behavior is abusive. It would be better to say:

> *"Mr. Smith, I want to help you in every way I can. You can help me to do that by using fewer four-letter words. That way, I can concentrate on helping to solve your problem, fair enough? I appreciate it."*

6. *"I have bad news."*

No matter how dire you believe your news to be, please don't preface the actual news with your judgment as to how bad the news is. You'll only be asking the client to perceive the news in as bleak a light as you see it.

Without a gloomy forecast, the listener might see clouds, but he or she will also see a number of silver linings. There are similar phrases to avoid that taint a listener's perception of the news to follow. One of my favorite no-no's is:

"You're not going to like what I have to say . . ."

I would also avoid using a popular cousin to this line:

"I have good news and bad news: which would you like to hear first?"

7. *"There are no exceptions."*

Have you heard the expression that says "For every rule, there is an exception"? Or possibly you've heard someone say, "That's the exception that proves the rule." Both of these truisms are well-known to your customers, so when they hear you proclaim there aren't any exceptions, their "B.S. Alarms" go off, and you lose credibility instantly.

If a customer badgers you, "Can't you make an exception?" try this reply:

"I wish I could help you that way, but I just couldn't explain it to my boss, who would see it as a good reason to fire me. Sorry, but let's see what we can *do, shall we?"*

If this is too lengthy, you could simply ask: "You wouldn't want me to lose my job, would you?"

8. *"You'll be treated like everyone else."*

Most of us are in favor of fairness—at least in theory. But we would actually prefer to be treated better than others, which actually is unfair as hell. The desire to be pampered is the secret behind the success of VIP lounges at airports, as well as the American Express Platinum Card (which currently costs $300 per year just to carry).

9. *"Life isn't fair, Mr. Jones!"*

Does he really need us, the people he does business with, to remind him of this philosophical truism? This kind of line makes us inherently sound superior because it summons to mind a teacher-and-pupil relationship. We cause resentment when we overtly try to change how someone thinks and feels.

10. *"Are you ready to be civil?"*

This is another superior-sounding comment that says: "You've blown your cool, Mr. Jones, but I haven't." This kind of snippy line simply prolongs hostilities.

11. *"I didn't make the policy."*

True enough, but this sounds like a tailor-made cop-out. This phrase won't persuade your client to treat you with more respect. If anything, some will interpret this as a gap between you and your firm, into which they can drive a wedge.

"We're Out of Stock."

Many of the toughest communications really involve us in managing disappointments. We need to soften the blow, whenever and however we can, while not losing a person's business. This can be tricky, particularly if we're explaining a situation that inherently portrays us as being incompetent. The out-of-stock scenario is one such situation.

Let's say a customer orders a widget from a company, but by the time the order is to be filled, it is discovered that there are no widgets in stock. At first glance, it seems the company isn't on top of the inventories, or purchases have been miscalculated. Either way, how can someone handle this without sounding like a bozo?

In such a situation, you employ the sequence used with the late-shipment situation, discussed earlier. You want to first apologize or empathize; second describe the problem and its cause; third predict when fulfillment of the order will occur; fourth indicate that you'll try to avoid this inconvenience in the future; and fifth thank the customer for his or her patience and business.

"Hello, Mary? How are you? Good. I'm calling to let you know that, unfortunately, the widget you ordered is temporarily out of

stock. Our computer showed more inventory than we had on hand when we last spoke. I've reordered a supply of widgets and we're going to have yours delivered by overnight mail when we get it. I expect you'll have it as early as Tuesday morning. Again, I apologize, and I don't expect this will happen again, OK? Thanks for your patience, and thanks for doing business with us, Mary. Bye."

The speaker also did something extra in trying to satisfy the customer. Did you pick up on the fact that the company is going to use overnight delivery to expedite the process when the widgets come in? This is just a symbol of the speaker's concern that the company avoid inconveniencing the customer any further.

The speaker could have chosen another gesture to make the same point. For example he or she could have said:

"In appreciation for your patience we're going to add some nice jumbo markers to your order at no charge, to say thank-you for doing business with us, OK?"

I received terrible service one evening at a usually wonderful restaurant. At the end of the meal, I mentioned this to the manager, because I didn't want to repeat the experience or write his place off of my list. As I was leaving the parking lot, the same manager unexpectedly knocked on my window and asked me to stop. Breathlessly, he apologized for the poor service, and then handed me a bottle of my favorite sparkling wine.

I appreciated the gesture so much that I returned the following week, bottle in tow, and enjoyed much better service. He kept my business with this relatively inexpensive symbol of appreciation.

"We've Had a Price Increase."

It's a fact of life that in most situations prices rise along with inflation. These added costs of doing business can either be absorbed by vendors or be passed along to customers. If we pass them along, we can maintain profit margins. If not, our profits shrink.

Therefore, it pays to devise diplomatic ways to persuade clients to accept price hikes. As I will indicate in the Postal Service illustration in Chapter 8, one of the best ways to take the sting out of price increases is by predicting them. This is valuable because it allows customers to stock up at lower prices. It also precludes them from expressing shock when the adjusted prices are put into effect.

Before getting into the exact language to use, it would be beneficial to discuss some of the facts of economics that most customers are at least implicitly aware of:

- Vendors can offer top-quality products.
- Vendors can offer top-notch service.
- Vendors can offer the lowest prices.

But as a general rule vendors can't offer the best products *and* the best service at the *lowest* possible prices. In other words, something has to give, and clients should be "psychologically adjusted" to *gently* and *agreeably* appreciate this truth.

If you think I'm kidding, just look at McDonald's. McDonald's is a spectacular success story. It provides the same food, at a modest price, with the same taste, with all due speed, nearly everywhere on the planet. But as one of my professors observed: "You won't find gourmet food at McDonald's, but they won't poison you, either." This firm does not deliver great quality, but it has good quality. Its employees don't deliver exceptional service, but they are generally competent and reasonably friendly. McDonald's delivers decent food at low prices in a clean environment. If that's what you expect, you will never be disappointed.

If McDonald's wanted to substantially hike up their prices, they would also be expected to raise their food quality or their service as a justification. Very small increases, periodically instituted, wouldn't appear on their customers' "radar" unless at the same time competitors slashed their prices and announced this fact through advertising.

Customers Realize They Can't Get the World for Nothing

Again, customers secretly know these economic truths, especially if they are also in business. They don't expect the world for a song, though they may pretend to as a negotiating ploy.

I did this the other day at the car wash. My cars needed to be detailed, which runs anywhere from $65 to $125 where I live. I asked the fellow who runs the detailing shop how much he charged for his work, and he replied, "$125 per car."

I said, "Gee that's high."

"Where can you get it for less?" he challenged.

"At ABC Detailing, at Pacific and Broadway. They do my cars for $75." (It's true.)

"Oh," he said, nodding his head. Then, in a whisper, he conceded, "We're higher here."

I couldn't believe it! Instead of justifying his premium price, he assumed that all detailing is equivalent in quality. Like most human services, there is a broad range of competence, and I hadn't been happy with ABC Detailing. They did their work with "a lick and a promise." So, for what little value they delivered, *they* were actually the high-cost vendor. If the car-wash fellow had simply reminded me of this fact, I would have respected him and caved in and paid his price. After all, I wanted to sell one of my cars, and what difference does $50 make if it helps me market the car for hundreds more?

Dash the Idea That Your Prices Are Too High

We should be prepared to utterly and enthusiastically defeat the contention that our prices are too high. There is a "shorthand" comeback to this objection, that salespeople are taught: price isn't value. This means that clients may find lower prices, but quality, service, or other expectations that they bring to their purchases won't be fulfilled. In other words, if they snap up the lure of a low price, the overall value they'll derive will diminish.

Justifying Higher Prices

How can you feel justified in charging higher prices? I mentioned already that your costs may have risen, requiring you to pass them along in one form or another. Or your profit-making requirements may have increased. You may work for a public company whose stock price will rise or fall according to reported quarterly earnings.

What did I just say? You need more profits? Isn't that greedy? Absolutely not. Profit is a necessary condition for staying in business. To think otherwise is to be naive. If you don't have profits, you don't have an incentive to go into or to stay in business. Without profits, there is generally no growth in opportunities for anyone, including yourself. No new jobs open up, no promotions occur, except through attrition, and the pie shrinks for everyone.

Customers also suffer because your firm can't be counted on to consistently deliver benefits. For example, I was a regular at a restaurant that served a wonderful, fresh vegetable soup. It was unlike any other. This establishment wasn't profitable, and after a few years of limping along, it went bankrupt. I would have gladly paid another 20 percent or even 25 percent for my meals to keep the restaurant in business!

Healthy profit margins are good signs of vitality, and they are the engines that propel us into a positive future. So don't be timid as you prepare to announce price increases. They are a necessary fact of life.

Now that we've established a psychological framework, let's turn to the language you can use to announce price increases.

How to Communicate Price Increases

Some increases we can merely announce. Others require explanations. Here is the general rule of thumb:

If the increase is very modest—only a few cents on the dollar—then a casual announcement should be all that you need.

"Hello, Bill? It's Gary Goodman with Goodman Supplies. How are you doing? Good. How's your stock of widgets—about how many do you still have on hand? Sure go ahead and look. . . .

"You only have about a dozen? Well, you're going to run out of those in about a week or so, right? OK, let's get you a reorder of six dozen, and those will be coming to you at $36.50 per dozen, OK? Great, and is there anything else I can help you with?

"Well, thanks for your business, and I'll talk with you soon. Bye."

Note that I didn't explain or justify the cost of the widgets. I just mentioned the price at which they would be "coming in." Usually, this is all you'll need—a casual notification, if the price hike is modest.

What do we do if the price increase is substantially more? If the increase is substantial and sudden, you'll need to explain and to justify the increase. Here's how to do it, embedded within the context of an order:

"Hello, Bill? It's Gary Goodman with Goodman Supplies. How are you doing? Good. How's your stock of widgets—about how many do you still have on hand? Sure go ahead and look. . . .

"You only have about a dozen? Well, you're going to run out of those in about a week or so, right? OK, let's get you a reorder of six dozen, and those will be coming to you at $46.50 per dozen. That's a little higher than what you've been paying in the past. The manufacturers have been passing along their higher prices because of the latex shortage, so it's a good idea to get in a supply now. And is there anything else I can help you with?

"Well, thanks for your business, and I'll talk with you soon. Bye."

What would have happened if the speaker didn't deliberately mention that the new price is higher than what Bill has been paying? Bill probably would have gone into sticker shock. This is what you feel when you've been hit with an unexpected and unexplained high price.

In this illustration, the speaker announces that the price is higher than what the customer has been paying, in order to prevent appearing like he's pulling a fast one on the customer to get away with something unfair. And tagged onto this announcement is the reason for the increase, i.e., that the manufacturer is passing along its higher costs for latex.

But there's also a little flourish thrown in that is worth noting. The speaker follows the announcement and the justification with the statement that it's "a good idea to get in a supply now." This implies that the price hikes may not be over. It keeps the door open for passing along more increases in the near future.

One more thing: This example gives the customer a rationale for seizing the new price instead of shopping with the competitors. This is critical. You don't want to lose anyone's business because of a poorly worded message.

"You Must Pay a Restocking Fee."

One of the most volatile issues in customer service is charging restocking fees for items that customers order, but then return to you for a hoped-for full credit. Product returns usually result from customers buying more of an item than they need. When they find they aren't reselling or using the item, they come for a refund or its equivalent. This is a problem for you, because the order and its partial or complete return has prompted several things to occur.

To fill the original order you went to the bother and the expense of gathering, shipping, and billing for the items. You may have extended credit as well, which means that you have paid the interest for the customer.

Moreover, when the customer drew down your inventory, you probably replenished your own supply. This involved coordination, computer entry, and finance costs. You also had to find a place to warehouse these items.

Now you will have to receive, unload, and account for the return. These activities involve labor and other costs.

Therefore, having to restock an item involves a lot of work and expense. This gives rise to the question: who should pay for these additional costs?

There are two ways to pass these costs along: you can accept returns without exacting a fee, and spread these costs across all customers, including those who never put you to the expense of processing returns; or you can charge only those customers who make you handle returns.

Choose the policy that you think makes more sense. There is something to be said for both options. (Read the Case in Point about Nordstrom's return policy on page 123.)

Now that this has been said, how do you persuade a customer to pay a restocking fee, which frankly, few people want to pay?

Take the approach that the restocking fee is really minor, which is to say, simply announce it at first, without launching into a complete justification:

"Mr. Smith, we'll be happy to help you in any way we can. In the matter of this return, there will be a modest 4 percent restocking

CASE IN POINT

Nordstrom

Nordstrom department stores are well-known for delivering a consistently high level of customer service. Part of their legend is that they'll almost always accept returns with few, if any, questions asked. And they'll credit customers with the full purchase price.

I interviewed a number of sales associates from my local Nordstrom store and asked them if they found there were customers who abused the privilege.

"Of course," they replied. "But even if we think so, we usually honor their requests."

How can Nordstrom do this? They can do it because they charge premium prices for their wares and there is enough profit left over, after they provide good service, to make their shareholders happy.

Generally, Nordstrom doesn't issue partial credits, or assess a service fee for handling returns. In their case, the good customers pay the way for any freeloaders. Is this fair? Again, you and your company need to decide.

By the way, there is another dimension to Nordstrom's apparent generosity. Let me present it to you in question form. Assume you work for Nordstrom and a customer wants to return an obviously timeworn shirt to your department. What will be a smoother and less stressful transaction for you and for the customer: offering a complete refund, or trying to negotiate a partial refund?

It's easier to say yes than to say no, don't you agree? So you may want to delve into the topic of how your company wishes to handle returns and other issues, from a *policy* standpoint. Whether you decide to assess fees for returns or not, you should be unified in your approach and feel convinced that you're doing the right thing.

fee that will be charged to your account, and is there anything else I can help you with?"

There it is in plain words. Note that the speaker still pays attention to the emotional agenda by prefacing the fee announcement with the statement that "we'll be happy to help you in any way we can." In keeping with this empathic mood, the speaker then describes the fee as "modest," which it is. This gives the customer a frame of reference to evaluate the magnitude of the fee.

Then comes something very important: an offer of further assistance. By adding the phrase "and is there anything else I can help you with?" several critical things are accomplished all at once.

The speaker implies having been *helpful.* This is good for customers to hear, because it is true. Regrettably, not enough customers appreciate this fact unless it is subtly pointed out. Remember the speaker said "we'll be happy to help" at the beginning? This was another seed the speaker planted to give the impression of being helpful.

The "and is there anything else . . ." phrase also smoothly implies: "This discussion point is over with—do you have any comments?" If the customer responds with a "no," they've implicitly agreed to accept and to pay the restocking fee.

And this same phrase gives customers a realistic chance to question the fee or to ask another unrelated question. This is an important provision because it assures the customers that we won't simply roll right over them with our announcement.

What if they take advantage of the opportunity to speak and they ask, "Why is there a restocking fee?" In this case, bring out the PEP format.

"Well, we have a modest restocking fee because it enables us to recapture some, but not all, of the costs that we've incurred by handling the same items twice. It also encourages our customers to plan their purchases so they don't end up overstocked or understocked. We believe it is more helpful than promoting a rule that all sales 'are final.'

"So, that's why we have a modest restocking fee, and is there anything else? Well, thank you again for doing business with us. Bye."

My consulting clients rave about this reply. I hope you have the same good luck when you use it. I believe it works because it sounds reasonable, doesn't it? After all, the speaker does offer three logical reasons to support the point. The speaker calmly says there are extra costs the company needs to defray. He or she also places responsibility upon the customer for having overordered to begin with. And the ultimate point is the most fun. It very nicely says, "Look—it could be *worse*. You could be required to keep and pay for everything!"

This hypothetical customer was informed about the fee, and then he asked for a justification, which was provided through PEP format. At the end of the fee announcement the speaker asked, "and is there anything else I can help you with?" Then, after the PEP talk, the speaker used a shortened form of the same question to bring things to a close: "and is there anything else?"

You might have wondered, "Isn't that needlessly repetitious?" It serves the important purpose of saying: "We've satisfactorily answered *that* question." By using it, you'll find you'll save everyone's time and be able to move on to the next issue or to the next customer.

"I Can't Help You Right Now!"

We want to help everyone as speedily as we can, but sadly, we can only assist one client at a time. This means we need a diplomatic way to create a waiting line.

After a client explains the problem, I suggest you use these words:

"Sure, I'll be happy to help you with that, but I'll need to call you back within the hour. At what number can I reach you? Great, I'll call by 4:00, and thank you for your patience. Bye."

This line sounds a lot more agreeable than simply saying, "I'm busy with another customer—can I call you back?"

The first phrase does several things. It says "You will get help, and I'll be happy to give it to you." This calms the client right away by forecasting a positive result. The phrase also says you personally take responsibility for helping. In other words, the client has found the right person and knows you'll be pleasant about it, because you're happy to help.

Then, you firmly say, "but I'll need to call you back." This is an assertive line through which you take control and set the agenda. It shows leadership, and most clients will yield to it.

Next, you tell the client as precisely as you can *when* to expect to hear from you, and how. This is comforting and gives closure to someone who could otherwise doubt your sincerity. You check the correct phone number, reinforcing your intention to continue the conversation, and end by thanking the person for his or her patience.

It's a neat and tidy way of saying, "I can't help you right now."

"You're in Breach of Contract."

I have had the pleasure of offering my seminars through thirty-five universities, coast to coast. The people with whom I've coordinated my programs have been forthright and honorable.

With one notable exception. I scheduled a program with one college where the administrator and I agreed to a reasonable, yet motivating compensation package. If enrollments were at twenty-five or below, I would receive a flat fee. For each enrollee above twenty-five, I would be paid an extra spiff of $22 per person.

When I arrived at the campus, the administrator greeted me and handed me a check for the flat-fee amount, despite the fact that we had forty registrations. I said "Thank you, but I think there's been a miscalculation." I reminded him of our agreement regarding extra compensation for extra registrations. He said the flat fee was "fair" and that it "should be enough." Obviously, he was going back on his word. What could I do? And how could I do it diplomatically?

I knew enough business law to recognize a breach of contract. This occurs when one party (or sometimes both) doesn't deliver, or threatens to not deliver, what was promised. There is a legal remedy. If you prove your argument before a judge, you'll probably be entitled to compensation.

But here's the rub: in America, in much litigation dealing with general contract law, each party is required to pay its own costs of prosecuting or defending a suit. Therefore, if someone aces you out of a small sum—say a few hundred or even a few thousand dollars—it might cost you more to recover your loss than the case is worth.

Consequently, there is a great disincentive to immediately threatening: "I'll sue you!" The other party could call your bluff and retort: "Go, ahead!" and where would that put you? It takes a lot of time and effort to wrangle, and as any lawyer will warn, *you may lose the case.*

So it's important to see the big picture and to realize that mere threats are quite limited in their effectiveness and can even boomerang. We need a diplomatic way to assert our rights and those of our company.

Here's how I handled the administrator's breach. We sat down and I said:

> *"Bill, I remember that we agreed to a spiff for every registration over twenty-five, and I was counting on this when I agreed to do the seminar at your campus. I believe in the sanctity of contract. If we agree to something, it's just not fair to unilaterally change it later on."*

I just closed my mouth after that. Instead of pushing the matter further, he backed down and paid me my due. What happened afterward was most surprising.

The seminar went exceedingly well and he invited me back to do another one, which I did, with the same positive result. Thus began, as Claude Rains said to Humphrey Bogart in the movie *Casablanca,* a great friendship.

Bill and I never argued about money again, and he became a strong booster of my programs. Our discussion of the misunderstanding cleared the air, and to this day, I believe he respected the fact that I stood up for myself.

Let's review the bullet points that were in my statement to Bill:

- We agreed to a certain compensation package.
- I relied upon this agreement in coming to his campus.
- Contracts are special and shouldn't be violated.

These could easily be rolled into a PEP talk, right?

> *"Bill, I should receive the extra spiff for each registration over twenty-five. We agreed to it; I relied upon it; and contracts*

shouldn't be violated. So, I should receive the extra spiff, Bill. Don't you agree?"

Use Tie-Downs to Cement Quick Agreements

Did you notice the extra flourish at the end? I asked: "Don't you agree?" In persuasion, we call this a tie-down. It can be a very useful tool to generate superquick agreements.

To see what I mean, let's return to the last PEP example. Yes, I could have ended it in the conventional way by declaring, "So I should receive the extra spiff." But in many cases, this kind of finale won't put your argument over the top and persuade your listener.

The tie-down provides an extra push and actually gets the other person to endorse what you've said. If you don't tie down your views in this way, you might leave the door open to a counterattack.

Here is a sampler of tie-downs you can use:

- *"That's nice, isn't it?"*

- *"Sounds good, doesn't it?"*

- *"So let's do it this way, fair enough?"*

- *"This should work well for both of us, OK?"*

Each tie-down operates according to people's tendencies to respond reflexively when we use certain phrases. For example, if someone says to you, "Let's go to dinner and then to a movie," you might respond, "No, let's go to a movie and then to dinner, OK?" This is much more likely to evoke consent than leaving your statement on a contrary note without a tie-down attached.

"You're Lying!"

You've probably noticed that some people seem to have two different value systems: one for their personal lives, and another for their business affairs. The same individual may never lie to her or his family but think nothing of telling mistruths in business situations.

I sell a number of products and I usually ship them via second-day mail service. It is a cheap and extremely reliable method, and it enables me to get products into my customers' hands quickly, while keeping their delivery fees quite low.

I've hardly ever had a delivery problem when I've used the U.S. Postal Service. But once, I mailed a set of tapes to a fellow in the Midwest who later claimed he hadn't received them. I sensed he was lying. Had he been telling the truth, he probably would have called me a week after he had placed his order, to ask me where his tapes were. I had to call him to find out why he hadn't made his payment. When we spoke, he was utterly unconvincing, and I offered to ship him another set, to which he replied, "No, that's OK."

To this day, I think he ripped me off! What could I do? I decided not to do business with him again. Moreover, I reconsidered the idea of sending return-receipts with my packages, but I decided it was too cumbersome from a paperwork standpoint, and it would add needless expense for my *honest* customers. I also reinstituted an advance-payment requirement for new buyers.

But with respect to this one rip-off artist, I let it go. In fairness, I suppose I could have been wrong. His tapes might have been way-laid, and he may have simply lost interest in getting them by the time we spoke again. But I don't think so.

There are several things that you can consider doing or saying when you think you've been lied to. You can simply chalk it up to experience and realize that, in the words of former Federal Reserve Chairman Paul Volcker, "If you're in business, you're going to have some bad debts." Or you can erect barriers to rip-offs, much like I considered requiring return-receipts for shipments. Inevitably, this will encumber your business, so you always have to ask yourself if the policing costs are more expensive to you and your customers than suffering the occasional losses from rip-offs. Finally you can choose to confront your customers.

Let's discuss this third option, shall we? There are several ways to confront suspected offenders. You can do a role reversal. Explain the facts and then ask the offenders, "If you were in my shoes, how would you handle this situation?" If they all too quickly reply, "Well, I don't think you can do anything," I would try a follow-up question. "Do you think I should turn this over to the Postal Service for tracing?" If they squirm, you may have validated your suspicions. On the other hand, if they cheerily say, "Sounds like a good idea to me!" you could be dealing with someone who is telling the truth.

In the delivery scenario, you can give the offenders a way out—a way to save face. Ask them: "Is it possible that the package arrived, but it has been misplaced, or could it have been delivered to the wrong part of the building? Could you check for me, please?" This approach can also serve as a litmus test of their honesty. If they seem utterly put out by your request, they may be hiding something. Usually, customers can empathize with our plight, and they will at least do something to see if they can help to find a solution.

Using the "Could you check for me?" request, I've been able to get clients to find phantom invoices as well as other documents that I *know* were mailed or faxed. I sense that by indicating you aren't going to give up easily and write off the loss or accept the delay, less than forthright customers drop their pretenses and start cooperating.

"We're Substituting Automation for Human Help."

Do you remember when voice mail was first introduced? People were up in arms. They were very antagonistic about dealing with machines instead of with people. Many used to blurt out, "I don't want to deal with a (expletive) machine!"

Most of us have grown accustomed to these electronic sentries and message takers. In fact, when I'm leaving messages, especially for people with whom I haven't communicated before, I'll ask the secretary if I can be connected to voice mail.

How come? It takes an exact message, including my vocal tones. A mere mortal could never leave a message as rich in detail or in meaning. So there are advantages to using technology to speed up processes, and in some cases, to replace humans.

We are woefully inadequate in conveying the pluses of using technology, because we're usually so preoccupied by what are considered disadvantages. For example, let's say your company is automating account information so customers can call in, twenty-four hours per day, seven days per week, to confirm their balances or to make payments. A machine never sleeps. It never takes a holiday either. This means customers can get help whenever they need it—at least for routine transactions.

That's a very big plus. Possibly you remember the pre-ATM days when people were strictly out of luck if they needed some cash on a holiday. If the supermarkets were closed, which once served as after-hours banks, people were in big trouble. The ATM, which was also battled against by people who thought they would miss long lines, surly tellers, and bankers' hours, has eliminated that worry for millions of people. What a convenience!

Moreover, there are incidental benefits to ATMs. Folks don't have to carry around large wads of money. By being able to get only the amount they need, they have made themselves less subject to being robbed and to losing their cash. And one more thing: while their cash is in the bank, it usually earns interest.

This example may seem obvious to you now, but that's my point. After people begin using technologies, few ever want to live or work without them. Would people in the South give up their air conditioners?

Our challenge is to show clients how innovations are desirable, normal, and permanent. In other words, we need to persuade people to accept the introduction of technology by characterizing the benefits. My favorite car dealer is a total pro at doing this. When I complained about the new grille on a line of cars that he carries, here's what he confidently said: "It looks unusual to you now, but I'll bet in six months you'll get used to it, and if you're like most people, you'll actually come to like it!"

"No way!" I remember thinking at the time. But guess what? He was right!

Let's put the ATM illustration into a PEP format:

"ATMs may seem a little unusual now, but we're confident once you try them, you'll like them, because:

- *They give you twenty-four-hour access to your accounts seven days per week.*

- *They eliminate the long wait in line at the bank simply to make a deposit or withdrawal.*

- *They actually add to your safety by eliminating the need to carry around large sums of cash.*

"So we're sure once you've tried ATMs, you'll like them."

This kind of PEP talk can work to introduce nearly any form of automation, including the Internet. Let's say that your company has decided to substitute a web page for the gorgeous color catalog that you used to mail four times a year. I'd justify such a change in this manner:

"In the future, you'll be receiving far fewer mailings from us. (We figure you probably have enough stuff in your in-basket as it is, right!?) Starting next quarter, you'll be able to see our entire catalog on-line at: www.productsareus.org!

"This will benefit you in three ways: with a few clicks, you'll instantly be able to see our entire product line; you'll be able to place orders twenty-four hours a day; and you'll be seeing reduced prices because we'll be passing along more savings to you. So, this innovation will really be a big plus."

"Don't Yell or Use Four-Letter Words with Me!"

Customers, as well as bosses, subordinates, and peers can become verbally abusive in various situations. Generally, people swear at us because they are frustrated. They blame us for not giving them what they want. Some turn to verbal abuse when they fear they are not going to get what they want or believe they are being treated unfairly. Sometimes people are angry at others but choose to take out their hostilities on us.

You have several options for handling profanity. You can try to ignore it, hoping that it will lessen or that the transaction will come to a conclusion soon enough. This takes special patience and concentration. Many folks don't like this response because they fear that apparent inaction may encourage the person to keep using the same language in the future. In other words, if you're not actively discouraging the behavior, you're really encouraging it.

When a client becomes verbally abusive, you can turn the call over to a supervisor or to an associate. The simple act of introducing a new personality in the transaction is a viable strategy because it surprises the verbal abuser. The person, thinking he or she has a victim, now suddenly has to adjust to someone new. Usually this will calm the person down.

I do not suggest you punish the person by saying, "Look, if you're swearing, you can just talk to my supervisor!" This will probably make the person more hostile and more likely to perceive you and your company as being hostile. Just say, "May I ask you to hold for a moment? Thanks." Then brief your associate on the situation and pass off the call.

Another option is to metacommunicate with the person. Metacommunicating can be literally translated as above-communicating. It is like opening a new channel—a higher channel—to get through to a person.

Specifically, metacommunicating is talking about the way we're talking, in order to improve how we're talking. For example, noting that a conversation is careening dangerously out of control, you might say:

"Bill, both of us seem to be raising our voices here. Let's see if we can bring the volume down a notch or two, fair enough?"

You can use the same device to bring attention to the annoying use of four-letter words:

"Mary, I have to admit that I have difficulty concentrating on the business at hand when I hear so many four-letter words. If we could limit the number of them, I think I would be more effective in doing a good job for you, OK?"

This is a lot different than shouting back: "You can't get away with swearing at me, buddy!" not to say, much more effective.

I would be less than complete if I didn't mention the ultimate alternative: you can *fire* the customer. Of course, I realize that this seems radical at first, but it may be necessary. If you have used every other device that your fertile imagination supplies, and the customer is still abusive, you have to reconsider the value of the person's business. I have fired more than one customer, and I must say, it has been most effective.

It enabled me to turn my attention to better business sources, and I have to admit that it brought a smile to my face. After all, I drew the line, they crossed it, and they were sent away. Frankly, it reminded me of the fact that *I* run my business, and it serves more than the interests of one client at a time. I simply can't surrender its control to an individual customer, nor can I afford to live in fear that I'll answer the phone and he or she will be on the other end.

One of my own better clients once mentioned this to me about his company's philosophy: life is too short to have to put up with unpleasant people—at least for long!

"You're Fired, Mr. Customer!"

So how should we fire our customers? Regrettably, we can't flare out at them and expect not to get burned. We need to maintain our civility, so at least *we* will feel good about the parting of the ways.

Recently I fired a client this way:

> *"Carl, I regret that I'm not going to be able to meet your requirements for doing business. I'm sure you'll find a source that will work out better for you, and I wish you much success. Goodbye."*

What's missing from this message? Details, for one thing. I didn't get into the fact that he swears and I can't stand it, or that he wants to haggle over prices every chance he gets. In effect, I placed the "blame," if you could consider it such, upon *me*. I said: "I regret that I am not going to be able to meet your requirements for doing business." I know it sounds as if I've failed him—that I'm not deserving of his business. So what? If these words make him feel OK about walking away, I have met my objective.

But what if he misses the point or misunderstands what I have said? Then, I'll be crystal clear:

> *"Carl, what I mean is this: you expect to be able to swear and carry on when you call us and we aren't comfortable doing business that way, so we're asking you to find another supplier, OK? Good luck to you, and no hard feelings. Bye."*

"Your Payment Is Late."

Next to telemarketing, the least enjoyable customer service function might be having to collect money from past-due customers. I have good news for you. It's not that difficult or even uncomfortable. My first full-time corporate job was in collections, so I'll show you how to do it without shedding needless tears.

First things first. Tell yourself the following again and again: it's not my money that's at stake. Why would I ask you to start with this idea? If you mistakenly think that it's your own dollars that are on the line, you'll get too emotional about collecting them. You won't have what social scientists call *role distance*.

Role distance enables surgeons to perform under great pressure because they have been trained not to think that their patients' lives are completely in their hands. Novelist-turned-filmmaker Michael Crichton earned his M.D. degree at Harvard, before turning to writing as a career. He could always tell when a fellow student would make it as a surgeon. Crichton says, "Something clicks inside your mind," and from that point forward, he asserts, such a student doesn't see the patient as a fellow human being. People become projects and tasks, but not bundles of personality attributes.

This needs to happen when discussing money that is in arrears. It shouldn't be seen as an emotional issue, nor should the debtor be perceived as morally inept or undisciplined. Your task is to make it comfortable for the person to get back into the habit of paying your firm.

The way you accomplish this is by developing a payment plan. The very first step is to persuade the debtor to promise you to pay a certain sum by a definite target date. But as with so many delicate communications, you just can't say:

> *"Hello, Mr. Smith? Our records show you're behind in your payments. When can we expect to receive your next payment?"*

Yes, this communicates the vital facts, but does it motivate the person to pay up? Equally important, if he owes a dozen or more companies such as yours, will he pay your bill first? Not with those words.

You need to seem friendly, which is not a natural tendency. In interpersonal relationships, what do you do when you sense that another party is about to break up with you? You cool down and start withdrawing your warmth and affection. Why? Because you don't want to get hurt any more than you're hurt now. But there's a problem with this reflex. You can accelerate the cessation of the relationship by obviously limiting your commitment. The same dynamics pertain to business settings.

Have you ever heard of the idea that if we seem to expect great things from our kids, they'll try to live up to these idealized portraits? And the converse also applies. Treat a child like she or he is "the bad seed," and you'll harvest a bitter person. The same idea applies to business.

So how do you express some corporate warmth without getting overly involved yourself? It's not that difficult. Try this:

"Hello, Mr. Smith? This is Gary Goodman, with Goodman Communications. How are things with you? And how's business?"

"OK."

"Well, we were a little concerned because it seems you're about sixty days behind in your payments. We would appreciate it if we could see a payment by Monday. Can you arrange that for me? I appreciate it, and is there anything else I can help you with? Well, thank you for doing business with us. Bye."

What stands out for you in this talk? First of all, the speaker makes small talk. This is very different than the approach taken by run-of-the-mill collectors. I think they must have a Doberman pinscher in mind that they're imitating. The speaker asks, "How are things with you?" which is a folksy chitchat question. This sounds like a customer service call more than a collections call, right?

Then the speaker asks about "business." This should get the customer to say there are financial problems, if any exist. If not, she or he will probably respond, "Fine, and yours?" Either way, you may get vital information about the solvency of your customer.

Next, concern is expressed as a method of framing the fact that the customer's account is past due. This is a smooth and very agreeable way of sharing bad news. Then a request for payment is made, prefaced with "we-would-appreciate-it" language.

After obtaining a promise to pay, the collector asks: "And is there anything else I can help you with?" Why would a collector do this? You get a gold star if you thought, "Because, once again, it makes the call seem like a customer service transaction." That's the point to handling a collections call as suggested. You treat the customers as if they are still highly valued and capable of giving you profitable business in the future. You don't stigmatize them and treat them as if their accounts are criminally delinquent!

"You Can't Get Credit with Us."

What if the same past-due client responded to your offer of additional help with the line: "Yes, there *is* something you can help me with. I need to reorder another two gross of your widgets. Would you ship them to me right away, please?" This would certainly put you in a tough situation, right? On the one hand, you want to make more sales, but on the other, you don't want to commit to extend more credit to an account that isn't paying in a timely way.

I suggest a direct approach:

"Sure, I'll be happy to help you with that. We'll ship you two gross of the widgets. That'll come to $562.50. Would you prefer to do that COD, or prepay?"

"Can't you bill me?"

"Unfortunately, not when there's a past-due balance on the books. Once you take care of that, we'll be back to your regular net-thirty-day terms, OK?

There are a few useful persuasive devices embedded in these messages. In the first instance, you offer a choice: "Would you prefer to do that COD or prepay?" In selling terminology, this would be called an alternative close. It's like someone saying, "That's a beautiful dress in blue, or would you prefer the red?" The helper would be asking the customer to choose between something and something, and not between something and nothing.

I know, from decades of experience, that you'll get your way much more often when you offer a real choice instead of imposing a single solution upon a customer. In the collections scenario, offering a choice gives the customer the impression that he has power—that you haven't so restricted his choices that you are dictating how he must do business. Remember, you don't want him to take his business elsewhere if his only problem is that he's behind in a payment or two.

"We Blew It, but We Want Your Business, Anyway."

I was doing a fun mental exercise the other day, which involved me in writing down my five favorite movies. Among them were: *The Natural*, with Robert Redford; *Heaven Can Wait*, with Julie Christie and Warren Beatty; *It's a Wonderful Life*, with Jimmy Stewart; *Rudy*; and *A Little Princess*. (My daughter introduced me to this one!) The exercise asks you to consider what theme connects the movies together. Once you find that, you'll have some insight into your personality. Well, I did this, and it was very interesting.

Three of the five are sports stories, and I do like coaching and playing sports. But that didn't connect all five. Then it hit me. All five are about people who are given *second chances.*

Thinking further, I realized that this is a major theme in American life. America itself was founded by pilgrims who wanted second chances at life. So I believe that most of our customers are willing to extend a second chance to us—even if we screw up big time—because they believe in forgiveness, and they would seek it in our place.

There are two important requirements involved in eliciting forgiveness and a second chance: we need to act contritely, and we need to seem committed to reforming. This means we should admit to our errors and pledge not to repeat them. Easy, right?

Let's try it in an example:

"Hello, Martha? It's Gary Goodman with Goodman Communications. I want to personally apologize for screwing up your billing as we did. We really weren't trying to get paid twice! I realize that our error may have made you look bad over at your company, and I never want to put you in that position again.

"I would appreciate a favor from you."

"What's that?"

"I would like a chance to make it up to you and set things straight. We'll send you your next set of widgets at half off. We're willing to lose a little money to save a great customer, fair enough?"

You're probably seeing a pattern by now. This communication contains a lot of empathy: the speaker explains clearly that his company made an error, and he says his company wants to rectify things and redeem itself. In a sense, his communication follows a ritual order for evoking forgiveness and a second chance. How could people of goodwill resist such an overture?

"You Can't Speak to My Supervisor."

Why do customers insist upon being connected to supervisors? They are not getting what they want from the person they're dealing with, and they believe someone higher in the chain of command will cut them a better deal. Others have no confidence that the frontline representative can deliver what they need, because the person doesn't have sufficient knowledge or experience. Some people want to deal with a supervisor because they have a personality clash with the frontline representative.

Why do we usually want to prevent customers from instantly accessing supervisors? It's time-consuming, and it upsets our working routines. Administratively, it's much more efficient if customers deal with customer service reps.

So customers think it's more advantageous to communicate up the ladder, while companies try to push communications down the ladder. Let's address these views in greater detail. Could a customer be right that she or he would get a better deal from a supervisor? In some cases, the answer is yes.

The other day I needed to deposit a large check into my credit union. I went in, saw a teller, and as I made the transaction I asked, "When will this be credited to my account?" She replied, "There will be a nine-day hold on the check because it's out of state."

There had to be a misunderstanding, I thought. This check was drawn upon my own account at a major brokerage firm. The office I dealt with was local, but its funds were in New York. No big deal. A phone call could easily be made to verify that it was a good check. So I asked: "Would you please ask a manager about whether a hold will be necessary?" Without expressing disdain she promptly did it. Upon returning she said: "No hold will be necessary."

I did receive a more favorable decision from her supervisor. It paid off to ask. But this scene has one element that differs from many requests customers make along these lines. Can you tell what it is? Hint: did I ask to speak directly to her supervisor? No, I asked *her* to do it for me. How would she have reacted if I had demanded to go over her head? Imagine the scene.

She would have had to explain why a customer was demanding to communicate with a higher-up. In doing so, she might have felt her competence was being challenged, and her boss might have felt obligated to defend the teller's professional honor. Moreover, the sanctity of upholding a rule would have been in question, so the manager might have felt pressure to deny my request as a symbol of the institutional need to toe the line.

In other words, it could have become a much bigger flap than it was. You can do the same thing when you are in the teller's situation.

If a customer declares, "I would like to speak to your supervisor about this nine-day hold," you can volunteer:

"Sure, I'll be happy to ask about it for you. Excuse me, I'll be right back."

What can this accomplish? First, it keeps you on your customer's side. You're "happy" to help in this way, so this transaction shouldn't degenerate into a you-versus-the-customer issue. Second, you can get a faster verdict from your boss than the customer could get, given that the two would need to be introduced. Third, you'll save some of your manager's precious time.

What if you answer a customer service line, and the first thing you hear is: "I need to speak to a supervisor!" You can still use the promise of help, with some modifications:

> *"Sure, I'll be happy to help you with that, but I would like to have a chance to see if I can help you first, OK?"*

This will probably work 50 percent of the time. If someone insists: "No, I said I want a supervisor!" I would simply reply:

> *"Certainly, may I ask you to hold for a moment? Thank you."*

Obviously, the customer has a strong desire to be put through to a supervisor, and in that case, you should yield to it. In any event, you don't want to get embroiled in a spat about whether a customer has the right to speak to a supervisor.

"You'll Have to Speak to My Supervisor."

Sometimes, you'll find that you need to "T-O," or turn over, a reluctant customer or client to your supervisor. Customers may prefer dealing with you because they're used to you—you're a known evil to them. They could believe that you're easier to negotiate with than a superior would be in the same circumstances. Of course, they may really like you and have formed an attachment.

How can you turn them over to someone else, and be delicate about it? One way, is by making the change sound as if it's a reward:

> *"Mr. Smith, it may be advantageous for you to take this up with my boss, Marsha. She's in a better position to see the big picture, so to speak, and I think you'll be able to take care of this issue a lot faster with her. May I ask you to hold while I connect you?"*

Couched in these terms, who can say no? Well, I'm sure you can think of some "customers from Hell" who can do just that. So as an exercise, let's presume that the person responds this way: "Actually, I would prefer to handle this with you. I really don't want to have to repeat the whole story, you know?" How's this response?

"I completely understand. That's why I'll tell her the story in 'short-hand,' and that'll save time all around. One moment, please . . ."

"I Can't Give You a Refund."

Your company could have a policy that prohibits refunds. This runs against customers' and clients' expanding expectations that they'll be able to undo nearly any purchase, if they're not completely happy with it.

I bring this up because it's important for us to consider the trends that attract our customers and clients. The "guaranty" trend is definitely one of them. Frankly, guaranties are becoming a way of life in modern marketing, and they serve some quite useful purposes. Guaranties encourage people to buy quickly without fear of making indelible mistakes that will blot their careers, or errors that they'll rue for the rest of their days. From a sales standpoint, faster decisions are cheaper for the seller. If more buying decisions can be engineered in less time, we can lower our sales costs, which translates directly into higher profits.

The downside is if we use guaranties as persuasive shortcuts, we may not arouse a genuine and lasting sense of commitment in the buyers. Therefore, buyers who are lured by guaranties are much more likely to unwind deals than folks who are sold without them.

A guaranty can be effective because it symbolizes our confidence in our products or services. After all, would we offer guaranties if we didn't believe we deliver great value?

Some people, even if they're dissatisfied, simply won't bother to invoke the guaranties or even warranties to repair malfunctioning products, especially if they anticipate being hassled. For example, how many people are going to package and ship their bulky weight-lifting machines back to manufacturers, at their own expense? Betting against this probability, some companies make wildly generous sounding promises, which they realize few will try to make them deliver upon.

If your company offers an unconditional, money-back guaranty, then it should be honored, period. You'll find that trying to weasel out of one only confuses and angers customers, while placing reps in the difficult position of having to justify why they aren't living up to their company's promises.

Providing Refunds as a Matter of Law

If your firm hasn't offered a money-back guaranty, yet a customer still demands a refund, you need to do a little fact-finding before you decline the request. You need to ask, did the product perform as promised? Did it perform as a reasonable buyer would expect it to perform?

If you promised a benefit that you don't deliver, you could be on the hook to either come through and make good on the promise or offer a refund—*as a matter of law.*

There is also an "implied covenant of merchantability and use" that is read into many purchases by the courts. In effect, it says that if we sell air conditioners, they should deliver cool air. If they don't, we have breached an implied covenant. Of course, if we promised "the coldest air you can get," and it blows hot air, we have violated an expressed covenant, and we're liable to the customer to make good one way or another.

Conditional Assurances

However, if you are in a situation where your firm has extended a *conditional* guaranty, then you'll want to exercise judgment. For example, let's say someone has purchased a machine from you, and it comes with a 90 day, parts-and-labor warranty, which has been clearly spelled out in writing. The customer, toting the document, requests a free repair 180 days after making an original purchase.

In this case, the customer has not satisfied one of the basic conditions of the warranty—presenting a covered repair request within 90 days. In this case, you should say:

"I appreciate your interest in getting this repair covered under warranty, but the warranty expired 90 days ago, and unfortunately, we aren't permitted to honor it. I'll be happy to give you the lowest price that we have on the repair, and if you're interested, I can put you in touch with a firm that sells extended warranties, so you might be able to avoid this situation in the future."

"Let's *Not* Do Lunch."

Socializing, as a part of doing business, is a delicate matter. You may be in an industry where you're more or less expected to have lunch with clients. Perhaps there are even events scheduled after hours, at conventions or at trade shows that your clients would like you to attend. How can you turn down these requests without offending people who are, at least indirectly, putting food on your table?

You could thank them for their invitations, but cite your company's policy against fraternizing with clients. Or you could mention your own professional code of conduct that precludes such socializing. Unfortunately, your clients could retort that the events *are* business-related, and therefore, you're acting too legalistic and straight-laced.

My preferred mode is to make one of these excuses:

"I appreciate the invitation, but I really don't take a formal lunch, so could we handle this during a normal meeting time?"

"I appreciate the invitation, but after 6 P.M. I'm on 'family time.' And they get grumpy if I cut in on it, if you know what I mean. So can we handle this during a normal meeting time?"

Did you notice the use of the phrase "a normal meeting time"? What am I trying to convey with these words? That's right, "It's abnormal for me to meet with clients during these times you have suggested, Mr. or Ms. Client."

What if they try to shame you into doing it by implying that you're working banker's hours? I would respond:

"I was advised a long time ago by one of my managers that if I can't get my job done during normal working hours, I'm doing

something wrong. I've taken that to heart, so let's find a mutually agreeable time for us to handle this."

This statement refers to an unnamed manager, who seems to have authorized your working day as you have constituted it. Often, a simple reference to an official-sounding third party will be enough to get the time-grabber off your back.

"Stop Flirting with Me!"

The lunch or dinner meeting request could be a thinly disguised attempt to ask you out on a date, or to develop a private relationship. In other cases, your clients could be flirting with you to see if you're available for companionship.

How can you discourage flirting? A good way to do it is by bringing attention to it with a direct question:

"Are you flirting with me, Mr. Jones?"

This should be enough to get the person to reflexively reply, "Why, no, I'm not!" You can move on without missing a beat:

"Very good, let's get back to business. . . ."

What if the person replies, "Well, golly, I guess I am flirting. You're so nifty!"? You can say:

"I'm not comfortable with that, so let's get back to business. . . ."

Do you have to disclose your marital or relationship status? Not at all, though you could say, "I'm spoken for," or "Thanks, but I'm married, so let's get back to business. . . ." It depends upon how much you wish to disclose.

There are indirect ways of discouraging flirtation, as well. You could mention your family, your spouse, or your significant-other during the course of a conversation, and the flirt may get the cue to back off. Or you could alert one of your colleagues to the situation and have them work your unavailability into a conversation.

Whatever you do for a living, you still have a right to a personal life that is *private*. You don't have to let anyone move in on this turf.

"Dear Customer—You're Demoted."

We already discussed how to fire a customer, but what if you only wish to demote them by taking away some of their privileges? Believe it or not, this can be a lot harder to do.

I belong to most of the frequent-flier clubs offered by major airlines. If you fly nearly all the time, many will bestow a special gold-card status upon you. This means that you'll earn more bonus miles and be able to get innumerable first-class upgrades. It's a nice package of goodies. And it's very hard to give up if your miles slip below a certain number. But that's what I had to do when I decided to curtail my travel. I had to relinquish my gold card.

What if you worked for the airline and you had to notify me that I was no longer entitled to my gold-card perks? How could you break the bad news without being shot?

I would recommend the "sandwich" approach, because it can soften the blow in this sensitive situation, as well as in others. Like PEP, it has three parts:

Start with good news.

"Hello, Dr. Goodman? This is Matilda with FaireAir. How are you doing? Great. I'm calling to thank you for your business over the years. We appreciate it."

I like the thank-you approach, because it starts a conversation on a very positive note. This tends to soften the blow of the negative information to come.

Next insert the bad news by sandwiching it between the good:

"I also want to see if your travel needs have changed—your frequent-flier account seems to have surprisingly few trips in it."

"Yes, I've cut back on my trips."

Finish with the good news, which in this case is a solution to the problem of losing one's "golden" privileges:

"Well, we would like you to once again enjoy gold-card status, and to reach that level you really won't need that many trips. About fifteen round trips will qualify. In the meantime, if we can help

you to plan any itineraries, please let us know, OK? See you soon. Bye."

This kind of call could certainly sound punishing if we didn't take care to use something like the sandwich approach. Let me mention one crucial element in this device: after we deliver the good news, then the bad, we absolutely must end on a positive note. Always finish with good news.

Some people have thought that a two-step, good news–bad news sequence is adequate, but it isn't. Almost always, it will leave the listener feeling disappointed from the high of the good news.

"We're Canceling an Event You Wanted to Attend."

Canceling a special event that you have been promoting to customers for some time can also be very disappointing. So how can you get away with it, without losing tons of goodwill?

> *"Mary, we really appreciate your business and your support over the years, especially with respect to attending our trade shows. That's why I wanted to get in touch with you as soon as I could. Unfortunately, we've decided to cancel the winter trade show in Honolulu."*

"You're kidding! Gee, we've been planning on that . . ."

> *"I know, so have I, and it wasn't an easy decision—at least from a personal standpoint. But from a business perspective, it just got out of control. We found we were subsidizing the show without getting nearly an adequate return, so our financial wizards pulled the plug.*

> *"I hope this won't cause you too much inconvenience. . . ."*

"Well, it's . . . a . . . nightmare. I was going to pull the kids out of school; Bill scheduled his vacation to coincide with the show; I put in for early vacation time; and we bought non-cancelable airline tickets . . ."

"I'm sure we're going to make this up to you, one way or another. I'll be happy to put our travel agent to work with your airline to see what we can do to get your money back. Would that help a little? And we can negotiate with the hotel so it will extend the same group rates to you, OK?

"In other words, we'll do whatever we can to help you not be out-of-pocket for this, fair enough? Again, I'm really sorry, and we'll make this up to you. Talk to you soon. Bye."

As you can see, when we cancel events, a constellation of consequences and complications arise for people who were planning to attend them. While from a strictly legal perspective we may or may not be on the financial hook for these problems, we should do whatever we can to lessen them. By promising to work with the airline and hotel, the customer service rep in the example attempted to do just that.

"Our Company Has Been Sold."

You've seen signs in countless restaurant windows that proclaim: Under New Management. These words can be a comfort to folks who hated the place before, and who may now give it a second chance.

But in many situations, when we have to break the news, or explain the reasons why our companies have been sold or merged, we are likely to disappoint our clients. They may have liked us as we were, and fear, rightly or wrongly, that we're going to lose all of the features that were attractive, while gaining no new benefits.

This happened to Glendale Federal Bank, which in its ads touted its personal service and small scale of operations as huge pluses. Glen-Fed also decried the impersonal aspects of larger, heartless banks. So it came as a shock to clients when a banking giant, California Federal, bought them out.

In this kind of situation clients are hungry for reassurance that they'll still enjoy service, convenience, and other perks. And this is a perfect time to make another sandwich.

"Hello, Gary? Hi, this is Nancy at GlenFed. How are you? That's good. How did that mortgage refinancing go for you? Good, I'm happy to hear it.

"By now, you may have heard that we've become a part of California Federal Bank, and I just want to let you know that we're going to be larger, but also better. I'll still be here at this branch, but you'll also get a chance to use CalFed's huge network of ATMs across the West. And we'll have other resources that can help your business to grow.

"So I wanted to share this with you and tell you how much I'm looking forward to working with you in the future, OK? Bye."

Summary

This chapter has focused upon what you can do to handle the twenty-one toughest client service situations. You've seen the PEP format in action, and you've been introduced to the sandwich approach for gently breaking bad news. You've also learned that there are several ways to retain your clients despite the fact that you're experiencing difficult times.

In the next chapter, you'll learn to communicate effectively with vendors and important outsiders. You'll be given methods for negotiating returns, replacements, discounts, and other accommodations. You'll learn some tips for doing damage control with the press. We'll also cover ways to maintain positive investor and community relations.

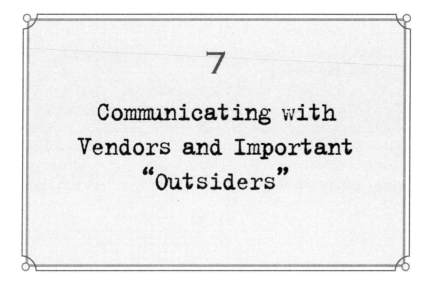

7

Communicating with Vendors and Important "Outsiders"

PREVIEW QUESTIONS

Would you like your vendors to give you first-class treatment and put you at the top of their customer or client lists?

Would you like to effectively negotiate returns, replacements, discounts, and other accommodations?

Would you like some simple language for getting people to willingly help you out?

Would you like to be able to handle the press during crisis situations?

Would you like to see how your company can maintain positive investor relations?

IN THIS CHAPTER you'll learn: to think like your vendors, so they'll give you the first-class treatment you deserve while putting you at the top of their lists; the best ways to negotiate returns, replacements, and discounts; a simple phrase to get people to help you out; to perform crisis management with the press; and how to improve investor relations.

How to Master Vendor Psychology

Vendors aren't from another planet. They think exactly as we do, only in reverse. So it shouldn't be difficult to figure out how to persuade them to want to deliver the best service to us and to our companies.

If there is one great secret to eliciting the best from our vendors, it is this: treat your vendors as if they were your customers! This sounds peculiar, at first. After all, aren't vendors supposed to treat *us* like the valued customers and clients that we are? Of course, they are. And they're more likely to do that if we show them some respect.

One thing we should do is respectfully consider their time to have as much value as our own. This means always return your vendors' calls, especially if they have responded to one of your inquiries.

For example, a client of six years asked me to come by to discuss formulating a training program for his firm. I arrived at the appointed hour, invested a good amount of off-the-clock time analyzing his situation, and was dispatched with an urgent request to E-mail a proposal within two business days.

I had to carve out a good block of my weekend time to make the deadline, yet I did it as an investment in our relationship. Four days later, I had heard nothing back. I left a voice-mail message and still got no reply. Only by probing the receptionist did I discover that my contact was going to be away for two weeks. He left me in limbo, holding a number of dates on my consulting calendar that I couldn't sell to anyone else until I had heard from him. All it would have taken was a clarifying E-mail or a return call from him, and I would have been able to carry on smoothly.

A wise person once said, "Rudeness in any form makes for a miserable association." With this thought in mind, I decided to decline the belated acceptance from the offending client, which arrived some two and a half weeks later.

The Etiquette of Dealing with Vendors

My client violated several points of business etiquette. These have existed largely as unwritten rules. We're going to explore them so you can avoid misunderstandings with your vendors.

When you have personally invited a businessperson to submit a proposal, you have a duty to be available, in a reasonably prompt time frame, to discuss the progress of the proposal. In fact, you shouldn't wait to be contacted. You should acknowledge receipt of the proposal and volunteer a time frame for its consideration. This reduces uncertainty and demonstrates respect for everyone's time.

Similarly if you have asked for an immediate or urgent response, one that calls for some degree of sacrifice on the part of a vendor, then an equally urgent response on your part is appropriate.

You also have a duty to help vendors reduce their sales costs. After all, they will pass along their costs to you in the form of higher prices, poorer service, and lessened responsiveness. How can you help them to cut costs? One way is by communicating quickly and directly when sellers *haven't* earned a sale.

I did this the other day after a speakers bureau had gone to some effort and expense to send me an informational packet. It was clear to me after having reviewed the materials that we didn't have a good fit. The first chance I got, I called the person who had signed the business letter, and said:

> *"Sally, this is Dr. Gary Goodman. I'm calling to thank you for sending me your packet. I don't think there is going to be a fit, but I want to save you the trouble of trying to follow up with me, OK?"*

"Sure, thanks for calling back."

"You're welcome. Good luck! Bye."

As a businessperson, I appreciate that countless millions of dollars are wasted in following up with dead leads. These are people who have either decided not to buy or are buying from someone else. Fearing confrontations and conflict, these folks will hide from unchosen suitors, hoping they'll finally get the message, give up, and go away. Generally, suitors are more tenacious than that. They won't give up until after they've played a lot of hide-and-seek with the prospective clients.

Businesspeople deserve a direct answer to the question, "Have I earned the privilege of doing business with you?" The faster we supply an answer, the better off we'll all be.

Every corporate CEO should audit the ways in which his or her employees deal with vendors. Many would be surprised to find their managers dispensing abuses to vendors while hoping at the same time that their own salespeople and representatives will be received with the utmost respect and dignity.

"What goes around, comes around" is an iron law of communication. Let's make sure we're sending politeness and etiquette to those we deal with. And a good place to start is by returning those phone calls, E-mails, and other messages. When we do, our vendors will take a lot better care of us.

How to Negotiate Returns, Replacements, Discounts, and Arrange Other Accommodations

There is one major tip I can impart to you about getting the best terms from your vendors. Simply put, it is this: don't sound like a lawyer as you approach these communications.

Let's say you run a boutique in a tourist town that gets most of its business during the Christmas holiday season. In September, you ordered a number of hats, including some fanciful, festive ones. Instead of arriving in late October, they didn't show up until just before Thanksgiving. Instead of being able to sell the four dozen that arrived, you would be lucky to sell two dozen.

From a strictly legal standpoint, you could probably rescind the entire deal, but this makes no practical sense. You do need *some* inventory. Moreover, you don't want to offend your vendor, who is the largest regional distributor of hats. What can you say to assert your interests, but still have a chance to sell as many hats as possible?

I would suggest this approach:

> *"Hello, this is Gary Goodman with Carmine's Boutiques. How are you? That's good. I'm facing a real problem, and I hope you can help me out."*

"Sure, I'll try to."

> *"That's great. As you know, I ordered four dozen hats back in September, with plenty of lead time for the holidays. Or so it seemed. The problem is that the hats just arrived on November 24th, and it's unlikely that I'm going to be able to move them all before the holidays, which is my season. What do you suggest I do?"*

"Do you want to return them?"

> *"Well, that's not going to work for me, unfortunately. I need inventory, but I can't afford to get stuck with excess stuff after the holidays. It'll hang around here for another year, if you know what I mean. Is there a way that you can discount them in place for me, so I can have less money tied up in them, and in that way lower my risk?"*

"How much do you have in mind?"

> *"I could handle them if you can discount the invoice by 35 percent, which comes to approximately $95. Can you do that for me? I would appreciate it."*

"I'll check into it and call you back."

This is anything but a hardball method of negotiating—it is like lobbing a huge softball at the vendor, who will feel inclined to take a cut at it. Why? It sounds human, and therefore it should evoke a humane response. Note how it begins: "How are you? That's good. I'm facing a real problem, and I hope you can help me out." These are magical words. Most people find being asked for help to be irresistible. They do promise to try to alleviate the problem when it is framed this way.

Instead of shouting, "You screwed me up by shipping these hats so darned late!" the speaker doesn't assign blame at all. The vendor knows she or he messed up, so the speaker doesn't need to rub it in. He is giving the vendor a chance to act magnanimously and to be heroic.

There's always time to argue contract law, if you have to. But make it your third or fourth strategy, certainly not the first.

How to Do Crisis Management with the Press

What can you do if you or your company is the subject of an embarrassing story in the press? Run and hide? You may feel like it, but this isn't the best way to do damage control. Often the best way is by becoming even more accessible, while promoting a definition of the situation.

Many of the techniques that we've covered in this book can come to your aid. The PEP format is excellent for responding to questions on the spot. It will make you seem utterly thoughtful and organized, even if you feel scattered and hopelessly short of time to prepare. If you're at a press conference, it can provide the glue that will make your replies seem coherent.

The sandwich approach can help you to acknowledge that matters have gone somewhat awry, but also that remedial measures are being taken. For example, assume that you work for a chain of well-known restaurants. Suddenly, a number of patrons become ill with bacterial poisoning. While not lethal, it is certainly an uncomfortable malady, and the press has gotten wind of the story. They've phoned you for a comment.

Unless you do an effective job of damage control, your firm will lose millions of dollars worth of business each day from being tainted by a perception that its restaurant units are not healthful. Here is how you can approach the matter:

"We can confirm that there have been about a dozen reports of patrons reporting stomach discomforts after having visited restaurants in the Southern California area. We're actively tracking these complaints, and we're on the scene. Right now this seems to be isolated to one or two facilities, and we are systematically testing all relevant menu items. We expect to have more information about this situation by 4:30 P.M. this afternoon.

"We're committed to serving our customers and to providing you with the most accurate and up-to-date information."

"Have you closed the suspected restaurants?"

"I can't confirm that, however, we're prepared to do whatever it takes to restore complete service to our customers. If this means temporarily closing some operations, until they can be resupplied, we'll do it."

"The last time something like this happened, it was traced to bad beef. Do you suspect the beef again?"

"We're looking at everything. And we hope to know more by 4:30 P.M., so we'll talk with you then."

When dealing with the press in a potentially embarrassing situation, it's important to appear committed to doing the right thing to rectify or alleviate the situation. In the scenario, the spokesperson says that she or he will "do whatever it takes to restore complete service." This includes the possibility of temporarily shuttering some restaurant locations.

It's also important to buy time until the facts can be gathered. What you don't want to do is speculate about the nature of the problem, and thereby send out false information to the press or to the public. So when asked if it was the "beef again," the spokesperson didn't offer an opinion, but deferred to the fact that the company is "looking at everything."

Handling Skittish Investors

Investors are always vitally interested in tracking the performance of their holdings. Moreover, whenever possible, they try to gather information that will elevate their confidence in the investments they've made, or in those that they're considering.

If you need to communicate with investors, the most important thing to remember is to sell the long-term vision that your firm is pursuing. For example, if your company believes that businesses will be using new technologies for attracting customers, then financial expectations should be framed within this scenario. You don't want to get bogged down defending this quarter's loss.

So if investors ask: "When will the red ink disappear?" you could respond this way:

> "We believe paid advertising on the Internet will triple in the next year, and that it will be ten times as heavy in three years. Given that scenario, we're expecting to see profits within twelve to thirty-six months. But more important than short-term profits is the positioning that we're creating for ourselves in the new world of Internet advertising. We believe this will make our shares very attractive to institutional investors in the near-term, though for obvious reasons we can't pinpoint when that will occur."

If an investor shows impatience, he or she can be reminded about the type of investment he or she has made:

> "As an investment, our shares represent a long-term growth opportunity. You're investing in the growth of the Internet and in new communications technologies. These take some time to become popular, but once they are established, they generally do well. Radio, television, and cable were all growth industries at one time, and their shares seemed speculative then. But they've all grown and thrived. And we're assuming the same should hold true for Internet-related shares."

To sum up the message we need to send to investors: be patient. If we can persuade them to be comfortable with an enlarged time frame, we can buy ourselves enough time to meet and potentially exceed their expectations.

Summary

This chapter has shown you how to get vendors to put you at the top of their service lists. You've learned the best way to negotiate returns, replacements, discounts, and other accommodations. You've also learned how to do damage control with the press. And you've seen how to maintain positive investor relations.

In the final chapter, you'll learn the art of preventing communication mishaps and miscues, in order to discourage difficult situations before they arise.

8

How to Prevent Communication Mishaps and Miscues

Would you like a way to build up goodwill with customers just as you build up a bank account?

Would you like a surefire method for preventing customers from feeling they're being taken for granted?

Would it benefit you to have a way to safeguard your clients from the persuasion of your competitors?

Would you like a permanent way to get your customers to sing your praises?

Would it be valuable to have a method for assuring the growth of your business through referrals?

Would you like an easy way to keep your company's name in front of clients?

Would it be an advantage to have a systematic way to get advice from customers?

Would your clients appreciate being given special, exclusive offers on products or services?

Would you like a way to take the shock out of sudden changes in customer pricing or other elements of doing business?

Would your clients appreciate it if you and your company always sound exceptional over the phone?

IN THIS CHAPTER you'll learn: to build goodwill with clients; to prevent customers from feeling they're taken for granted; to discourage customers from using your competitors; to get your customers to sing your praises; to grow your business through referrals; to keep your company's name before your clients; to get great advice from your customers; to retain customers by giving them special offers and perks; to take the shock out of sudden price increases and unexpected changes; and twenty-one ways to sound exceptionally good over the telephone.

*   *   *   *   *   *   *

I hope that we've established at least one overarching point in this book: there are numerous ways to communicate your way through the most challenging business situations. Yet you're probably wondering, aren't there some equally valuable techniques for *preventing* problems before they occur?

Fortunately, there are, and we're going to explore them in this final chapter. I'm going to give you a ten-point prevention checklist of general business communication practices. This will be followed by twenty-one specific tips for smoothly handling your business interactions by telephone.

A Pound of Prevention Is Much Better than an Ounce

You've heard that an ounce of prevention is worth a pound of cure. That's true, but we shouldn't be satisfied with giving merely an ounce. What I mean is we should show as much sensitivity to customers when things are going well as we do when we suddenly find ourselves in trouble.

By trying to be great communicators as a normal part of our functioning, we'll earn what are known as "idiosyncrasy credits." These are like deposits in the Bank of Goodwill. Every time we extend a courtesy or surpass expectations, the value of this invisible account increases.

Likewise, when we screw up, customers draw down their balances. Our big errors and mishaps result in their major withdrawals. And if we force our customers to suffer through a succession of poor interactions, our funds might disappear altogether. Or worse still, our balance can even move into the red or be overdrawn.

Sooner or later, most of us will commit an error or have to break bad news to customers. When this happens, make sure to have enough deposits of goodwill to draw upon. If you do, you won't have to live or die based upon the eloquence of your sudden explanations.

Your Prevention Checklist

Here are ten everyday customer-service practices that will build your goodwill credits:

- *Thank your customers incessantly.*
  This might seem awkward, but we can't possibly overexpress our gratitude. By favoring us with their trade, customers believe they are

doing something important for us—and they are. So we should acknowledge it as often as we can.

What happens in intimate relationships when we forget to tell our counterparts how important they are to us and we take them for granted? That's right; their ties to us weaken, and the next suitor to happen along can woo them away.

We should go beyond thanking customers every chance we get. Actively pursue new ways to express gratitude. Send them postcards, give them free premiums bearing your company's name, and leave them positive voice-mail messages.

The need to do this is accentuated when buying cycles are long, since we wouldn't have natural opportunities to see or speak with our customer base. For example, I have been using an independent insurance agent to buy my car and office insurance. Frankly, he does a miserable job of staying in touch with me. The only time I see his name or hear from him is when I need to renew my policies or when the underwriters need some information from me, such as the mileage level on my odometer. Otherwise, he's a phantom.

This is problematic. Recently, I had to submit a claim, and he bungled the processing of it. I believe that he is so unused to dealing with customers by phone that he misinterprets what they want. If he were to stay in touch, it would make it easier to chat with him as well as to be understood. And of course, when he made errors, I would accept them with greater equanimity if he would occasionally thank me for my business.

- *Appear genuinely happy to help your customers in any situation.*

Have you ever noticed that most vendors will return your phone calls, nearly on the spot, if you leave them a message that says you want to buy an additional product or service? But how quickly will they reach for the phone if you say that you have a problem with one of their current products? That might be an entirely different story, right? Let's not follow in their footsteps.

Try to seem enthusiastic and equally available whether you're dealing with good news or bad news. In other words, make it easy for customers and clients to do an entire spectrum of business with you.

I bought a car a few years ago, which the foreign manufacturer asserted was the pinnacle of engineering achievement. In fact, I was sent a video that featured actual engineers touting how their autos "had backup systems for the backup systems." I kid you not—these were their exact words.

Well, the car was more than a lemon. It was a nightmare straight from the Black Forest! The "check engine" light was constantly on, even after I returned from frequent repair trips to the dealership. Every major system failed, including the brakes and the transmission.

This was a huge letdown. I was treated like a prince when I bought the car. They even presented me with two dozen long-stemmed red roses as I finished the paperwork! I was definitely given the "white glove" treatment.

But how did my old pals at the dealership respond, four months later, when I insisted they take the car back and give me a complete refund? They weren't nearly as warm, I'll tell you that. But they were still polite, and they did what they could to coordinate my negotiations with the local factory representative.

After two months of effort, I got my refund. Five years later, I went back to the same dealer and bought another new car, because they had done their best to seem genuinely happy to help me, in good times and in bad.

How can you be sure to convey this attitude? Practice listening to customer requests, and then, no matter how difficult or irksome the request, preface your response with these words:

"Sure, I'll be happy to help you with that."

Clients will not only appreciate this, but they'll see that you're open to communicating with them, come what may. That will distinguish you from the average fair-weather friend.

- *Every chance you get, ask if there's anything else you can do for your customers.*

Smart marketers have known for a long time that 80 percent of their sales will usually come from a mere 20 percent of their customers. This means that those who do business with us are probably our best sources of additional revenue and profits. Treat existing clients well, because they have the power to pay you back many times over.

You can perform a very positive customer service and marketing function at the same time. All you have to do is regularly ask this question before you conclude your conversations:

"And is there anything else I can help you with?"

This phrase opens the door to anything and everything. If folks are having a minor problem with your product or service, they'll probably tell you about it. Treat this as a good sign. If they didn't care about continuing to work with you, they would squelch their smaller problems and misgivings until they could identify a replacement vendor.

By eliciting all kinds of feedback with this phrase, you'll be able to nip problems in the bud. At the same time, you'll inevitably prime the pump so more business will flow your way. It's amazing how these words jog the memory, making customers recall, "Oh, yeah, there is something else I'm interested in."

By inserting this phrase at the end of all of your transactions, your customers will come away with this impression, which will distinguish you from other providers: "That person is so helpful!"

• *Ask how your service compares to others your customers do business with.*

By asking customers, "How do we rate when compared to others?" you will often get essential feedback about several things.

If customers aren't happy with something, they might respond: "I don't know about anybody else, but I am having a little problem with your widget." So your question is a reality-check for how your products are performing.

But you are also sending an important message that says, "We know you have a choice of providers, and we want to ensure that you'll keep choosing us in the future." You are saying you really care about their opinions.

Moreover, this question reveals to you the perspective your customer has regarding your competition. If they say, "I haven't worked with them, but I understand Acme might give you folks a run for your money!" you can bet that they'll contact Acme if or when you falter.

Such a customer reaction should also be your cue to investigate Acme and to perform a little competitive benchmarking. Benchmarking is the process of comparing your pricing and procedures to those of your industry colleagues. If you're way out of line, you can correct any major deviations and safeguard your customer base from your competitors.

- *Ask clients to write you a note about your service quality.*
There is a familiar expression that asserts, "If you really want to learn a subject, try teaching it." By taking on the greater challenge of teaching, you must master the lesser, but included, challenge of learning the subject matter.

A similar dynamic operates when it comes to creating lasting customer satisfaction. If we can persuade our customers to write a letter or even a brief testimonial quote that praises our efforts, they'll become anchored to the belief that we're supreme service providers. Because they're "on record" for supporting us, they'll be reluctant to withdraw their support in favor of another source. Additionally, we'll be able to use their praise in brochures and in other marketing channels. But what happens if they refuse our request?

Well, that can certainly be a sign that there's "trouble in River City"! While it's true that some firms have policies that preclude employees from providing endorsements, most do not. Someone's reluctance to recommend us in this way could very well indicate that they're less than pleased. We should take this as an opportunity to ferret out the reasons for the dissatisfaction and then address them immediately.

- *Ask customers to refer new business to you.*
Like asking for a testimonial, requesting a referral to customers' friends or associates can provide you with a litmus test of your customers' opinions of your service. If they're willing to risk their credibility by recommending you, you can generally infer that you're doing a good job. In fact, giving you a referral may be the highest compliment a customer can bestow.

The process of recommending you also recommits your customers to you. After all, it is cognitively inconsistent for them to refer a friend or a colleague, and then drop your services themselves.

- *Communicate with buyers frequently through various means, including newsletters. Also, make it easy for them to contact you.*
Keeping your name in front of your customers is very important, because it reminds them of who you are, and who they've chosen to do business with. Tests have shown that people who buy cars, for example, actively seek to read more ads for the model they've chosen, to bolster their prior decision to buy.

Don't make your customers work this hard! Send them newsletters that contain handy information as well as your company's logo. Develop an easy-to-use website so they can obtain information about you, twenty-four hours a day. These communications media will make you and your company seem accessible, while sending the message that you're open to their ideas and respectful of their needs.

• *Place your best customers on your advisory boards and panels.*
I write articles for a number of customer service and sales publications, and I serve on their advisory boards. They bring me their questions about various issues that they may not thoroughly understand. If they're planning to print a special issue, they'll often ask for my input before they commit resources to the project.

What do I get from these publications? Exposure is one thing. People see my articles and read my ideas on a regular basis. Periodically, they call me about giving a keynote speech, consulting, or obtaining my recorded training programs. Moreover, I derive prestige and status by serving on these boards. It makes me feel important—that I'm making a contribution and an impact.

A major Midwestern university has a very large advisory board, which is populated by numerous human resources managers from local companies. These executives are really the major buyers and influencers who are responsible for selecting training resources for their firms.

So who do you think they turn to when they suddenly have a need for a certain type of outside trainer or consultant? That's right, they call the university on whose advisory board they serve. When the university considers sponsorship of one of my courses, they don't rush to print and mail tens of thousands of brochures. They call a dozen of their key advisory board members and ask them if they'll commit to sending a certain number of folks to my program. If these board members are enthusiastic, the program is launched. If not, the university has saved a lot of time and money by not hosting it.

As you can see, it pays to invite your customers to serve on these boards.

• *Periodically send clients special coupons and exclusive offers.*
It is an established fact that coupons and exclusive offers bring in additional business, but we don't use them frequently enough.

This is especially the case when it comes to rewarding our existing clients.

Marketers invest small fortunes trying to attract *new* clients, and this seems logical—at least superficially. The reasoning is: Why invest in people who are already on board, buying from you week in and week out? Isn't that wasteful?

The answer is: Not at all. Retaining customers costs one-fifth of the price of obtaining new ones. But please note what I said. It does cost *something* to retain customers. Their continuing patronage isn't a free entitlement.

Give them periodic perks that say, "Thanks for doing business with us!" After all, this is the philosophy behind frequent-flier programs, right? Give them free miles, they'll reward us with their loyalty. Despite the fact that these reward programs have been phenomenally successful, most businesses haven't emulated this winning practice. They mistakenly think they deserve ongoing business because they once hustled and earned it.

The key is that we have to continue earning it. Special coupons, exclusive offers, and other rewards say we're willing to pay the price.

- *Be quick to alert customers to changes that will affect them.*

I have to tip my hat to the U.S. Postal Service (USPS), which used to be one of the most offensive agencies in this country. This behemoth has really started inculcating a customer service philosophy into its personnel, and it shows.

Now postal customers are given a great amount of lead time to adjust to looming postage increases. USPS sends out mailers to major users alerting them to pending increases. Moreover, it tries to take the sting out of price hikes by offering free direct-marketing seminars to teach participants how to mail more cost-effectively.

If you're in the shipping-supplies business, and you learn that the cost of paper is going to rise, doesn't it make sense to communicate this fact to customers before they flip out and complain, several weeks or months down the road? It's much easier to calmly predict what is going to happen, than to manically justify what has already occurred. Be a visionary for your clients—don't let them feel blindsided.

Commit Yourself and Your Company to Achieving Telephone Effectiveness

Apart from strictly retail transactions, where we hand over our money or plastic to actual clerks, more and more of our transactions are being done by telephone. I mentioned that my insurance agent was telephonically challenged, but he's not alone! Otherwise-capable people can and often do sound horrific over the phone. Largely because they have never heard their phone manners, they are unaware of how they are deficient. I suggest we start to remedy this situation by increasing everyone's awareness of the importance of telephone effectiveness.

I suggest you begin your improvement program by adopting these twenty-one tips for answering inbound calls. I've recommended them elsewhere, especially in my seminars and consulting, and they definitely improve the communication climate.

1. *Answer promptly.*

Few things irk people more than having to wait for a phone to be answered. If we subject a caller to a lengthy delay, he or she infers that we are too busy for him or her, or we are uncaring. By the time we do answer the line, the caller is fit to be tied.

Have we said anything to arouse the caller's wrath? Of course not. But his or her perceived poor treatment at our hands has already begun. Without knowing it, we've dug ourselves into a communication hole, which we'll need to climb out of once the actual conversation begins.

How many times should someone hear your phone ring before you answer it? No more than four times, whenever possible. Proper allocation of human resources should enable you and your firm to staff the lines to respond within this period. If you choose not to, then you're implicitly choosing to irritate callers and discourage future interactions.

2. *Pleasantly greet the caller.*

In some offices, it is customary for people to bark out only their last names as a way of greeting callers. You'll hear this a lot in military and law enforcement settings. As you can imagine, it sounds very unpleasant and unduly authoritarian and forbidding.

A better way is to announce your name, your department if necessary, and then to attach an offer of help, as in:

"Hello, Human Resources, this is Gary—how may I help you?"

3. *Use the caller's name.*

Most people appreciate it when they are spoken to as individuals. We can accomplish this by using their names every now and then in conversations. Beware of overdoing it, though. If you find yourself saying a person's name every other phrase, it's excessive, and it could backfire and seem manipulative.

4. *Apologize for delays or errors.*

If you asked a person to phone at a certain time, and she or he did but you weren't available, that would seem rude and it would require an apology. When connecting with the person again, you would be wise to mention how sorry you were, right away. This would clear the air and send a message that you are sensitive to the importance of that person's time.

5. *Use diplomatic responses.*

Gee, what are diplomatic responses? "Beats me!" (Obviously, this last phrase isn't one of them, right?) Diplomatic phrases sound smooth and pleasant. For instance, if we don't have the answer to someone's question, we would probably want to say:

"That's a question I would like to answer for you, but I don't have the right information. May I research that for you and get back to you?"

6. *Give the other party the option of holding or being called back.*

Forcing someone onto "hold" isn't very friendly. For example, I was stuck in traffic on my way to a meeting at a hotel. I decided to alert the person who was expecting me that I would be about twenty minutes late.

I called the concierge's desk, and she instantly tried to compel me into a holding pattern. "Concierge," she barked, "Can you hold?" which communicated, "You better say yes!" I said, "No, I can't!" as fast as I could. I went on to explain the message that I needed to get to her guest, who happened to be standing right in front of her at the time.

We should generously offer the choice of placing someone on hold or being called back. The concierge should have used a more pleasant and less rushed tone. She could have said:

"May I ask you to hold for a few minutes, or would you prefer I call you back?"

What a difference that would have made in my impression of the hotel!

7. Always fulfill a promise to call back.

This sounds fairly obvious, but many folks drum up excuses to avoid calling others back, especially after they've promised to do so. One excuse I've often heard is, "I didn't get the information I expected to give to the person I was calling, so I decided to wait until I had it." This won't wash. In such a situation, we should phone the person as early as possible, if only to apologize for not having the anticipated information. We should also make a firm prediction of when we'll have the data we need. If we don't call back as promised, we seem unreliable and we promote a less trusting communication climate.

8. Avoid abrupt questions and phrases.

"Could be." "Don't know." "Not sure." "Understood." All of these are abrupt phrases that can sound distant, uncaring, and somewhat evasive. Use full sentences, even if you intend to communicate exactly the same thing. For instance, "Well, that could be the case," sounds much more pleasant than the abbreviated version.

9. When taking the perfect message, note specifics.

The worst message is, of course, the one that we deliver verbally: "Uh, someone called, and I don't know who it was, but I think it was a guy." Talk about being vague!

We should try to get as many relevant specifics from the caller as we can. These include: his or her properly spelled name; the department or company from which the call is coming; area code and phone number; time zone, if the area code sounds unfamiliar; and a brief reason for the call.

If you want to get a gold star, you can agree to note the tone of voice of those who call for your associates, and they can do the same for you. This information can help your associates to emotionally prepare for what they expect to hear when returning the calls.

10. *Tell your coworkers where you are going if you have to unexpectedly leave your desk or office.*

This enables your coworkers to sound intelligent when speaking to people who call when you are away. You may not want your associates to reveal that you're at the dentist's office, but you can authorize them to indicate when you will be available.

11. *When an associate receives a call while on another line and you can see she or he is tied up, take the caller's name and put a note in front of the associate.*

You could just as easily transfer the call into voice mail, but if the call sounds urgent, your associate may want to know about it right away.

12. *Always say thanks and good-bye before ending the conversation.*

It's only polite.

13. *Don't hang up too quickly.*

This gives the other person a chance to offer a last-minute remark, or to ask a suddenly remembered question.

14. *Ask for feedback to ensure that the message you left was clear.*

This is the mirror image of my advice concerning taking a message. Make sure that the transcriber notes every aspect of the message you want to leave. I would use these words to check:

"Just to make sure I was clear, would you mind very much reading the message back to me?"

This makes the message taker feel that we're taking responsibility for the quality of the message, and not challenging his or her abilities.

15. *When disconnected, try to call back if you initiated the call.*

This will avoid lengthy delays that can occur when both parties expect the other to make the next move.

16. *Always be polite.*

Easy to recommend, but hard to do—at least when we're provoked. But I like to use this phrase at the end of difficult calls, "Thank you for your courtesy." Said nicely, it clears the air and restores ruffled feathers.

17. *Discontinue noisy activities when speaking on the phone.*
For example, refrain from chewing gum or eating lunch.

18. *Never leave the phone off the hook.*
It could be one of Murphy's Laws that the absolutely worst gaffe in the world will be heard by someone important when the phone is inadvertently left off the hook. Simply use the hold button if you step away from a call, and you'll avoid this problem altogether.

19. *Give the boss privacy when he or she receives a personal call.*
You're sitting in your boss's office. The phone rings, and your boss suddenly lights up and sounds chummy with the caller. If the call goes into what seems to be personal matters, gesture that you'll come back in a few minutes. If the boss overrules you and motions for you to stay put, that's OK. At least you've shown sensitivity.

20. *Discontinue conversations with associates when the phone rings.*
It's humanly impossible to simultaneously carry on two different conversations. (Just watch, now that I've said this someone will invent software to enable us to do this!) But it is important that when a call comes in and you've answered it, the call should take precedence over other conversations you might be having in the office.

21. *Use common sense.*
A philosopher said that common sense is the most uncommon thing of all! Nonetheless, I suggest you employ it as well as the golden rule when you communicate, not only by phone, but in all business-related situations: communicate with others as you wish them to communicate with you.

Summary

Remember this: there is always a tomorrow. When we communicate, we leave a legacy for ourselves as well as for countless individuals who will join the never-ending conversation later. Like a stream near a campsite, we should appreciate its beauty and potential for sustenance.

We should also do everything we can to avoid polluting our communications with needless incivilities and overt hostilities. I hope this chapter has shown you how to prevent misunderstandings and difficult encounters.

And I hope the prior chapters have provided you with new tools for communicating in difficult and unavoidable business situations. It has been my intention to offer concrete examples and real-world texts, as well as to give you the organizational tools for improvising on your own in situations not covered here.

I've enjoyed being your guide. Let me leave you with this thought. No matter how challenging the situation you find yourself in, there is *something constructive* you can say or do to make it better. Try to give it your best, even if circumstances occasionally seem bleak or hopeless, and I'm sure you'll amaze yourself with what you can achieve!

Afterword

THANK YOU FOR reading this book. I enjoyed writing it, and I hope you got a lot out of it. If you would like to learn more about my audio-cassettes, videos, or seminars and consulting, please contact me at the address below. In the meantime, good luck!

Dr. Gary S. Goodman
P.O. Box 9733
Glendale, CA 91226
voice: 818-243-7338
fax: 818-956-2242
E-mail: goodmanorg@earthlink.net

Index

Accountability, 32–33
Activating events, 6–7
Advisory boards and panels, 168
Anger, as response to conflict, 5–6
Apologies, 30–38
  and accountability, 32–33
  empathic nonapologies vs., 39–41
  as entitlements, 31
  and giving something extra, 34
  half-hearted, 31–32
  "I" vs. "we," 34–35
  impulse to avoid, 31
  and legal considerations, 38
  and professionalism, 33
  sincerity of, 32
  voice quality for, 35–38
The Art of War (Sun Tsu), 85
Assertiveness, 20–21
ATMs, 131–32
Attorneys, 89
Authentication, 21
Automation, introducing, 130–32
Avoidance, 5

Bad credit, communicating about, 137–38
Bad-news messages, delivering, 109–49
  avoiding pet peeve phrases when, 113–16

  about breach of contract, 126–28
  about cancellation of special events, 147–48
  about credit problems, 137–38
  and customers vs. clients, 111
  to demote the customer, 146–47
  to fire the customer, 134
  about flirting, 145
  about having to postpone assistance, 125–26
  about late payments, 135–37
  about late shipments, 112–13
  to lying customers, 128–30
  managing disappointments when, 116–17
  and offering a second chance, 138–39
  about out-of-stock items, 116–17
  about price increases, 117–21
  about refusing a refund, 142–44
  about refusing to socialize, 144–45
  about restocking fees, 122, 124–25
  about sale of company, 148–49
  about speaking or not speaking to supervisor, 139–42
  about substituting automation for human help, 130–32
  to swearing customers, 132–34
Bargaining. *See* Negotiating
Bargaining statements, 56–57